botanical knits 2

TWELVE MORE INSPIRED DESIGNS TO KNIT AND LOVE

By ALANA DAKOS of NEVER NOT KNITTING

NNK
PRESS

Copyright ©2014 Alana Dakos and NNK Press
Illustrations copyright ©2014 Neesha Hudson

First Edition / ISBN 978-0-9883249-4-7 / Paperback
First Edition / ISBN 978-0-9883249-5-4 / PDF

Library of Congress Control Number: 2014902638

Printed in China

Published by NNK Press / P.O. Box 1635 / Atascadero, CA 93423

Copy editing by Nicole Crosby
Technical editing by Tana Pageler and Dawn Catanzaro
Graphic design by Mary Joy Gumayagay

www.botanicalknits.com

table of contents

54

100

32

88

42

76

70

12

60

66

22

94

INTRODUCTION

The world of nature is a continuous source of inspiration for me. With the huge variety of plant life surrounding us, there are so many features to explore, concepts to try, and stitch patterns to play with. After the overwhelming response to my first book in this series, *Botanical Knits*, I felt a sequel publication was in order. Creating beautiful knitted items inspired by botanical elements is something I truly enjoy and feel can never be exhausted.

In this follow-up collection, traveling cables, organic textured stitches and lacy stitch patterns make a re-appearance. From the cables of a heavy sweater-coat to the delicate stitches of a lace shawl, the essence of plant life is worked into each of the 4 sweaters and 8 accessories included in this book.

Before you begin the pattern of your choice, please consider the following reminders.

MAKE CAREFUL DECISIONS BEFORE YOU GET STARTED

Choosing the correct size and yarn before you begin is essential for a well-fitting and attractive finished garment. Remember to carefully compare the measurements on the sizing schematic to your own body measurements, and choose a size based on how you want the sweater to fit. Most sweaters in this book are modeled with 2–3" / 5–7.5 cm of positive ease. If you are looking for a similar fit, a good rule of thumb is to choose a size with a bust measurement that is 2–3" / 5–7.5 cm larger than your own bust measurement. For a closer fitting sweater, choose a size with 0–2" / 0–5 cm of negative ease. Make good use of the included sizing schematics. These measurements will really help you determine how the particular design will look when worn.

A lot of attention has been given to fiber content and properties for the yarn chosen for these projects. For this reason, I suggest you use the recommended yarn brand whenever possible. If you are interested in substituting

a yarn, however, please choose one with a similar fiber content, and the same weight and gauge as the recommended yarn for the pattern. This will result in the best outcome.

ALWAYS CHECK YOUR GAUGE

When it comes to ill-fitting sweaters or accessories, inaccurate gauge is almost always to blame. For your own sanity, please take the time to check your gauge before you begin. An accurate gauge swatch should be at least 4" / 10 cm across. It should be bound off, washed, blocked and dried before measuring. Making a gauge swatch first is not a step to be missed. Just a little bit of inaccuracy in your stitch count can mean inches of difference in a finished knit.

If you prepare well before beginning your project, you will help to ensure the finished item looks and fits the way you envisioned. If you have questions or would like to share your experience of knitting items from the *Botanical Knits* collections with other knitters, please join the Botanical Knits group on *Ravelry*.

Every pattern in the *Botanical Knits* collection has been tested and checked for accuracy by multiple technical editors and test knitters prior to publishing. Despite our best efforts, however, sometimes errors can still slip by.

If you think you have found an error or have a question about a pattern instruction, please contact us by email at techsupport@nevernotknitting.com and be sure to visit www.botanicalknits.com/errata for pattern corrections.

I hope this sequel collection provides you with continued inspiration and hours of enjoyable knitting!

elana

SWEATERS

sprig

A top down, raglan pullover with striking details.
A small sprig of foliage adorns the asymmetrical neckband and sleeve cuffs.
Dart-like shaping is added to the bust and hips for a flattering fit.

Yoke

CO 22 sts onto circular needle. Do not join into the rnd.

Row 1 (WS): {P1, pm} twice, p18, {pm, p1} twice. Using backwards loop cast on method, CO 5 (5, 5, 6, 6)[6, 7, 7, 7] sts.

Row 2 (RS): Sl 1, {knit to marker, M1R, sm, k1, sm, M1L} twice, k1. CO 5 (5, 5, 6, 6)[6, 7, 7, 7] sts. 36 (36, 36, 38, 38)[38, 40, 40, 40] sts: 20 sleeve sts, 7 (7, 7, 8, 8)[8, 9, 9, 9] front and back sts, 2 raglan sts.

Row 3: Sl 1, purl to end. CO 5 (5, 6, 6, 6)[7, 7, 7, 7] sts.

Row 4: Sl 1, {knit to marker, M1R, sm, k1, sm, M1L} twice, knit to end. CO 5 (5, 6, 6, 6)[7, 7, 7, 7] sts. 50 (50, 52, 54, 54)[56, 58, 58, 58] sts: 22 sleeve sts, 13 (13, 14, 15, 15)[16, 17, 17, 17] front and back sts, 2 raglan sts.

Row 5: Sl 1, purl to end. CO 5 (6, 6, 6, 7)[7, 7, 8, 9] sts.

Row 6: Sl 1, {knit to marker, M1R, sm, k1, sm, M1L} twice, knit to end. CO 5 (6, 6, 6, 7)[7, 7, 8, 9] sts. 64 (66, 68, 70, 72)[74, 76, 78, 80] sts: 24 sleeve sts, 19 (20, 21, 22, 23)[24, 25, 26, 27] front and back sts, 2 raglan sts.

Row 7: Sl 1, purl to end. CO 8 (8, 8, 9, 9)[9, 10, 11, 12] sts.

Row 8: Sl 1, {knit to marker, M1R, sm, k1, sm, M1L} twice, knit to end. CO 8 (8, 8, 9, 9)[9, 10, 11, 12] sts. 84 (86, 88, 92, 94)[96, 100, 104, 108] sts: 26 sleeve sts, 28 (29, 30, 32, 33)[34, 36, 38, 40] front and back sts, 2 raglan sts.

Row 9: Sl 1, purl to end. CO 10 (10, 11, 11, 11)[12, 12, 12, 12] sts.

Row 10: Sl 1, {knit to marker, M1R, sm, k1, sm, M1L} twice, knit to end. CO 10 (10, 11, 11, 11)[12, 12, 12, 12] sts. 108 (110, 114, 118, 120)[124, 128, 132, 136] sts: 28 sleeve sts, 39 (40, 42, 44, 45)[47, 49, 51, 53] sts, 2 raglan sts.

Row 11: Sl 1, purl to end. CO 10 (11, 11, 11, 12)[12, 12, 12, 12] sts.

Row 12: Sl 1, {knit to marker, M1R, sm, k1, sm, M1L} twice, knit to end. CO 10 (11, 11, 11, 12)[12, 12, 12, 12] sts. 132 (136, 140, 144, 148)[152, 156, 160, 164] sts: 30 sleeve sts, 50 (52, 54, 56, 58)[60, 62, 64, 66] front and back sts, 2 raglan sts.

Row 13: Sl 1, purl to end. CO 12.

Row 14: Sl 1, M1R, pm, k1, pm, M1L, {knit to next marker, M1R, sm, k1, sm, M1L} twice, knit to end. CO 14.

Row 15: Sl 1, p1, pm, p1, pm, purl to end. CO 10.

Row 16: Sl 1, {knit to marker, M1R, sm, k1, sm, M1L}, rep 3 times more, knit to end. CO 18. Do not turn. Join into the rnd by knitting to next marker, sm, k1, sm. This is now the beg of the rnd. 200 (204, 208, 212, 216)[220, 224, 228, 232] sts: 34 sleeve sts, 64 (66, 68, 70, 72)[74, 76, 78, 80] front and back sts, 4 raglan sts.

Next rnd: Knit.

Inc rnd: {M1L, knit to marker, M1R, sm, k1, sm}, rep 3 times more. 8 sts inc.

Rep last 2 rnds 7 (9, 11, 13, 15)[17, 19, 21, 23] more times. 264 (284, 304, 324, 344)[364, 384, 404, 424] sts: 50 (54, 58, 62, 66)[70, 74, 78, 82] sleeve sts, 80 (86, 92, 98, 104)[110, 116, 122, 128] front and back sts, 4 raglan sts.

Cont in St st for 3 rows more. Yoke measures approx 5 (5½, 6¼, 6¾, 7¼)[7¾, 8½, 9, 9½]" / 12.5 (14, 15.5, 17, 18.5)[20, 21.5, 23, 24.5] cm from initial CO sts on left (longer) sleeve.

DIVIDE FOR SLEEVES

Next rnd: *K80 (86, 92, 98, 104)[110, 116, 122, 128], remove marker, slide 52 (56, 60, 64, 68)[72, 76, 80, 84] sts on a holder, using backwards loop method, CO 4 (6, 8, 10, 12)[14, 16, 18, 20] underarm sts; rep from * once. On last rep, pm in the middle of the underarm sts for the new beg of rnd. 168 (184, 200, 216, 232)[248, 264, 280, 296] sts.

Work even in St st for 3½" / 9 cm from underarm.

Set up rnd: K21 (23, 25, 27, 29)[31, 33, 35, 37], pm, k42 (46, 50, 54, 58)[62, 66, 70, 74], pm, k49 (54, 58, 63, 68)[72, 77, 82, 86], pm, k28 (30, 34, 36, 38)[42, 44, 46, 50], pm, k28 (31, 33, 36, 39)[41, 44, 47, 49].

Dec rnd: {Knit until 2 sts rem before marker, ssk, sm, knit to next marker, sm, k2tog} twice, knit to end. 4 sts dec.

Rep dec rnd every 6 rnds 4 times more. 148 (164, 180, 196, 212) [228, 244, 260, 276] sts.

Cont in St st for 13 rnds more.

Inc rnd: {Knit to marker, M1R, sm, knit to next marker, sm, M1L} twice, knit to end. 4 sts inc.

Rep inc rnd every 4 rnds 5 times more. 172 (188, 204, 220, 236)[252, 268, 284, 300] sts.

Work even until body measures 14½ (14¾, 15¼, 15¾, 16¼)[16½, 17, 17½, 17¾]" / 37 (37.5, 38.5, 40, 41.5)[42, 43, 44.5, 45] cm from underarm.

Purl 1 rnd.

Knit 1 rnd.

Rep last 2 rnds twice more.

BO all sts purlwise.

Left Sleeve

Divide 52 (56, 60, 64, 68)[72, 76, 80, 84] held sts evenly among dpns. Pick up and knit 6 (8, 10, 12, 14)[16, 18, 20, 22] sts from CO at underarm, pm in the middle of the picked up sts to mark beg of rnd. 58 (64, 70, 76, 82)[88, 94, 100, 106] sts.

Knit 3 rnds.

Dec rnd: K1, ssk, work until 3 sts rem, k2tog, k1. 2 sts dec.

Rep dec rnd every 14 (8, 6, 6, 4)[4, 4, 2, 2] rnds 4 (6, 10, 10, 8)[16, 16, 6, 12] times more, then every - (10, -, -, 6)[-, -, 4, 4] rnds - (1, -, -, 5)[-, -, 13, 10] time(s) more. 48 (48, 48, 54, 54)[54, 60, 60, 60] sts.

Work even until sleeve measures 10½" / 26.5 cm from underarm. Cut yarn.

LEFT SLEEVE CUFF
NOTE: Cuff is worked over sts on dpn. At the end of each RS row, the last cuff st is worked together with 1 or 2 live sleeve sts using a ssk or sssk, thus binding off the sleeve sts. It is beneficial to work the first few stitches on the RS rows loosely to keep the I-cord edging from becoming too tight around the arm.

CO 4 sts onto dpn.

Rows 1 and 3 (WS): Sl 1, p1, sl 2.
Row 2 (RS): K3, ssk (one sleeve st with one cuff st).
Row 4: K3, sssk (two sleeve sts with one cuff st).

Work rows 1–4 0 (0, 0, 1, 1)[1, 2, 2, 2] time(s) more, then work rows 1–3 once more.

Work rows 1–51 of Chart A.

Rows 1 and 3 (WS): Sl 1, p1, sl 2.
Row 2 (RS): K3, sssk.
Row 4: K3, ssk.

Work rows 1–4 0 (0, 0, 1, 1)[1, 2, 2, 2] time(s) more, then work rows 1 and 2 once more.

Work either Regular Cuff or Button Loop Closure.

REGULAR CUFF
Purl 1 WS row.

BO all sts.

With yarn tails stitch CO and BO edge together.

BUTTON LOOP CLOSURE
Work in I-cord for 8 rows. Cut yarn, leaving a long tail. Thread tail onto tapestry needle, pass through rem 4 live sts and cinch to close. Use yarn tail to secure end of I-cord next to beg of cord on the edge of the cuff to form a button loop. Sew on buttons opposite button loops.

Right Sleeve
Work as for left sleeve to the cuff.

RIGHT SLEEVE CUFF
NOTE: Right sleeve cuff is worked in the opposite direction as the left sleeve cuff so that they are mirror images of each other. At the end of each WS row, the last cuff st is worked together with 1 or 2 live sleeve sts using a p2tog or p3tog, thus binding off the sleeve sts. It is beneficial to work the first few sts on the RS rows loosely to keep the I-cord edging from becoming too tight around the arm.

CO 4 sts onto dpn.

Rows 1 and 3 (RS): Sl 1, k1, sl 2.
Row 2 (WS): P3, p2tog (one sleeve st with one cuff st).
Row 4: P3, p3tog (two sleeve sts with one cuff st).

Work rows 1–4 0 (0, 0, 1, 1)[1, 2, 2, 2] time(s) more, then work rows 1–3 once more.

Work rows 1–51 of Chart B.

Rows 1 and 3 (RS): Sl 1, k1, sl 2.
Row 2: P3, p3tog.
Row 4: P3, p2tog.

Work rows 1–4 0 (0, 0, 1, 1)[1, 2, 2, 2] time(s) more, then work rows 1–3 once more.

Work either Regular Cuff or Button Loop Closure as for Left Sleeve Cuff.

Finishing
NECKBAND

With circular needle and RS facing, beginning at center of longer sleeve, pick up and k9 sts along CO edge of sleeve, 56 (58, 60, 62, 64) [66, 68, 70, 72] sts along front section, 32 sts along second sleeve section, 56 (58, 60, 62, 64)[66, 68, 70, 72] sts along back section, 9 sts in sleeve section to where you began. 162 (166, 170, 174, 178) [182, 186, 190, 194] sts. Cut yarn. Tie ending yarn tail to CO yarn tail to secure in place.

NOTE: Neckband is worked over sts on a dpn as for left sleeve cuff, binding off neck sts at the end of RS rows using a ssk or sssk.

CO 5 sts onto dpn.

Row 1 (WS): Sl 1, p1, sl 3.
Row 2 (RS): k4, ssk.

Rep last 2 rows 4 times more.

Row 1 (WS): Sl 1, p1, sl 3.
Row 2 (RS): K4, m1-p, ssk. 6 sts.
Row 3: Sl 1, k1, p1, m1-p, sl 3. 7 sts.
Row 4: K3, p1, k1-tbl, p1, ssk.
Row 5: Sl 1, k1, p1, k1, sl 3.
Row 6: K3, p1, k1-tbl, pfb, ssk. 8 sts.
Row 7: Sl 1, k2, p1, kfb, sl 3. 9 sts.
Row 8: K3, p2, k1-tbl, p1, pfb, ssk. 10 sts.
Row 9: Sl 1, k3, p1, k2, sl 3.
Row 10: K3, p2, k1-tbl, p3, ssk.
Row 11: Sl 1, k3, p1, k2, sl 3.
Row 12: K3, p2, k1-tbl, p3, sssk.

Rep last 2 rows 4 (4, 5, 5, 6)[6, 7, 7, 8] times more.

Row 1 (WS): Sl 1, k3, p1, k2, sl 3.
Row 2 (RS): K3, pfb, p1, k1-tbl, p3, sssk. 11 sts.
Row 3: Sl 1, k3, p1, k3, sl 3.
Row 4: K3, p3, k1-tbl, p1, pfb, p1, sssk. 12 sts.
Row 5: Sl 1, k4, p1, k3, sl 3.
Row 6: K3, p3, k1-tbl, p4, sssk.

Rep last 2 rows 7 (8, 8, 9, 9)[10, 10, 11, 11] times more.

Work rows 1–64 of Chart C.

Row 1 (WS): Sl 1, k11, sl 3.
Row 2 (RS): K3, p11, sssk.

Rep last 2 rows 4 (5, 5, 6, 6)[7, 7, 8, 8] times more.

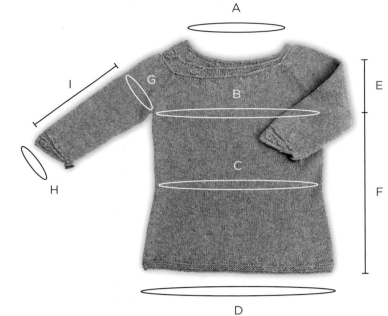

A	Neck circ	26½ (27, 27½, 28¼, 28¾)[29¼, 29¾, 30½, 31]" 67 (68.5, 70, 71.5, 73)[74.5, 76, 77.5, 78.5] cm
B	Bust circ	33½ (36¾, 40, 43¼, 46½)[49½, 52¾, 56, 59¼]" 85.5 (93.5, 101.5, 109.5, 118)[126, 134, 142, 150.5] cm
C	Waist circ	29½ (32¾, 36, 39¼, 42½)[45½, 48¾, 52, 55¼]" 75 (83.5, 91.5, 99.5, 107.5)[116, 124, 132, 140] cm
D	Hip circ	34½ (37½, 40¾, 44, 47¼)[50½, 53½, 56¾, 60]" 87.5 (95.5, 103.5, 112, 120)[128, 136, 144.5, 152.5] cm
E	Yoke depth	6 (6½, 7¼, 7¾, 8¼)[8¾, 9¼, 10, 10½]" 15 (16.5, 18, 19.5, 21)[22.5, 24, 25.5, 27] cm
F	Side length	15 (15¼, 15¾, 16¼, 16¾)[17, 17½, 18, 18¼]" 38 (38.5, 40, 41.5, 42.5)[43, 44.5, 45.5, 46.5] cm
G	Upper arm circ	11½ (12¾, 14, 15¼, 16½)[17½, 18¾, 20, 21¼]" 29.5 (32.5, 35.5, 38.5, 41.5)[44.5, 48, 51, 54] cm
H	Cuff circ	9½ (9½, 9½, 10¾, 10¾)[10¾, 12, 12, 12]" 24.5 (24.5, 24.5, 27.5, 27.5)[27.5, 30.5, 30.5, 30.5] cm
I	Sleeve length	10½" / 26.5 cm

Row 1 (WS): Sl 1, k11, sl 3.
Row 2 (RS): K2, ssk, p10, sssk.
Row 3: Sl 1, k10, sl 3.
Row 4: K3, p10, sssk.
Row 5: Sl 1, k10, sl 3.
Row 6: K3, p3, p2tog, p5, sssk.
Row 7: Sl 1, k9, sl 3.
Row 8: K3, p9, sssk.
Row 9: Sl 1, k9, sl 3.
Row 10: K2, ssk, p8, sssk.
Row 11: Sl 1, k8, sl 3.
Row 12: K3, p8, sssk.
Row 13: Sl 1, k8, sl 3.
Row 14: K3, p4, p2tog, p2, sssk.
Row 15: Sl 1, k7, sl 3.
Row 16: K3, p7, sssk.
Row 17: Sl 1, k7, sl 3.
Row 18: K2, ssk, p6, sssk.
Row 19: Sl 1, k6, sl 3.
Row 20: K3, p6, sssk.

Rep last 2 rows 4 (4, 5, 5, 6)[6, 7, 7, 8] times more.

Row 1 (WS): Sl 1, k6, sl 3.
Row 2 (RS): K2, ssk, p5, sssk.
Row 3: Sl 1, k2, k2tog, k1, sl 3.
Row 4: K3, p4, sssk.
Row 5: Sl 1, k4, sl 3.
Row 6: K2, ssk, p3, sssk.
Row 7: Sl 1, k3, sl 3.
Row 8: K3, p1, p2tog, sssk.
Row 9: Sl 1, k2, sl 3.
Row 10: K2, ssk, p1, ssk.
Row 11: Sl 1, p1, sl 3.
Row 12: K4, ssk.
Row 13: Sl 1, p1, sl 3.

Rep last 2 rows 10 times more.

BO all sts.

Stitch cast-on and bind-off edges of neckline together using yarn tails.

Weave in all ends on the WS. Wet block to measurements.

Chart A

Row 1 (RS): K2, M1-p, k1, sssk.
Row 2 (WS): Sl 1, M1, p1, k1, sl 2.
Row 3: K2, p1, k1-tbl, p1, ssk.
Row 4: Sl 1, k1, p1, k1, sl 2.
Row 5: K2, pfb, k1-tbl, p1, sssk.
Row 6: Sl 1, kfb, p1, k2, sl 2.
Row 7: K2, p2, k1-tbl, p2, ssk.
Row 8: Sl 1, k2, p1, k2, sl 2.
Row 9: K2, pfb, p1, k1-tbl, p2, sssk.
Row 10: Sl 1, k2, p1, k3, sl 2.
Row 11: K2, p3, k1-tbl, p2, ssk.
Row 12: Sl 1, k2, p1, k3, sl 2.
Row 13: K2, p1, pfb, p1, k1-tbl, p2, sssk.
Row 14: Sl 1, k2, p1, k4, sl 2.
Row 15: K2, p4, M1R, K1-tbl, p2, ssk.
Row 16: Sl 1, k2, p2, k4, sl 2.
Row 17: K2, p3, Right Leaf B, k1-tbl, p2, sssk.
Row 18: Sl 1, k2, p1, k1, p3, k3, sl 2.
Row 19: K2, p2, k2tog, k2, p1, k1-tbl, p2, ssk.
Row 20: Sl 1, k2, p1, k1, p3, k2, sl 2.
Row 21: K2, p2, k1, k2tog, p1, k1-tbl, p2, sssk.
Row 22: Sl 1, k2, p1, k1, p2, k2, sl 2.
Row 23: K2, p2, k2tog, p1, k1-tbl, p2, ssk.
Row 24: Sl 1, k2, p1, k4, sl 2.
Row 25: K2, p4, k1-tbl, p2, sssk.
Row 26: Sl 1, k2, p1, k4, sl 2.
Rows 27-38: Rep rows 15–26.
Row 39: K2, p1, p2tog, p1, Inc-3, p2, ssk.
Row 40: Sl 1, k2, p3, k3, sl 2.
Row 41: K2, p3, k3, p2, sssk.
Row 42: Sl 1, k2, p3, k3, sl 2.
Row 43: K2, p1, p2tog, k1, k2tog, p2, ssk.
Row 44: Sl 1, k2, p2, k2, sl 2.
Row 45: K2, p2, k2tog, p2, sssk.
Row 46: Sl 1, k3, k2tog, sl 2.
Row 47: K2, p2tog, p2, ssk.
Row 48: Sl 1, k3, sl 2.
Row 49: K2, p3, sssk.
Row 50: Sl 1, k2tog, k1, sl 2.
Row 51: K2, p2tog, ssk.

Chart B

Row 1 (WS): P2, M1, p1, p3tog.
Row 2 (RS): Sl 1, M1-p, k1, p1, sl 2.
Row 3: P2, k1, p1, k1, p2tog.
Row 4: Sl 1, p1, k1-tbl, p1, sl 2.

Row 5: P2, kfb, p1, k1, p3tog.
Row 6: Sl 1, pfb, k1-tbl, p2, sl 2.
Row 7: P2, k2, p1, k2, p2tog.
Row 8: Sl 1, p2, k1-tbl, p2, sl 2.
Row 9: P2, kfb, k1, p1, k2, p3tog.
Row 10: Sl 1, p2, k1-tbl, p3, sl 2.
Row 11: P2, k3, p1, k2, p2tog.
Row 12: Sl 1, p2, k1-tbl, p3, sl 2.
Row 13: P2, k1, kfb, k1, p1, k2, p3tog.
Row 14: Sl 1, p2, k1-tbl, p4, sl 2.
Row 15: P2, k4, p1, k2, p2tog.
Row 16: Sl 1, p2, k1-tbl, M1L, p4, sl 2.
Row 17: P2, k4, p2, k2, p3tog.
Row 18: Sl 1, p2, k1-tbl, Left Leaf B, p3, sl 2.
Row 19: P2, k3, p3, k1, p1, k2, p2tog.
Row 20: Sl 1, p2, k1-tbl, p1, k2, ssk, p2, sl 2.
Row 21: P2, k2, p3, k1, p1, k2, p3tog.
Row 22: Sl 1, p2, k1-tbl, p1, ssk, k1, p2, sl 2.
Row 23: P2, k2, p2, k1, p1, k2, p2tog.
Row 24: Sl 1, p2, k1-tbl, p1, ssk, p2, sl 2.
Row 25: P2, k4, p1, k2, p3tog.
Row 26: Sl 1, p2, k1-tbl, p4, sl 2.
Row 27: P2, k4, p1, k2, p2tog.
Rows 28-37: Rep rows 16–25.
Row 38: Sl 1, p2, Inc-3, p1, p2tog, p1, sl 2.
Row 39: P2, k3, p3, k2, p2tog.
Row 40: Sl 1, p2, k3, p3, sl 2.
Row 41: P2, k3, p3, k2, p3tog.
Row 42: Sl 1, p2, ssk, k1, p1, p2tog, sl 2.
Row 43: {P2, k2} twice, p2tog.
Row 44: Sl 1, p2, ssk, p2, sl 2.
Row 45: P2, k3, k2tog, p3tog.
Row 46: Sl 1, p2, p2tog, sl 2.
Row 47: P2, k3, p2tog.
Row 48: Sl 1, p3, sl 2.
Row 49: P2, k3, p3tog.
Row 50: Sl 1, p2tog, p1, sl 2.
Row 51: P2, k2tog, p2tog.

Chart C

Row 1 (WS): Sl 1, k2, kfb, k1, p1, k1, kfb, k1, sl 3. 14 sts.
Row 2 (RS): K3, p4, M1R, k1-tbl, p5, sssk. 15 sts.
Row 3: Sl 1, k5, p2, k4, sl 3.
Row 4: K3, p2, Right Leaf A, k1-tbl, p5, sssk. 17 sts.
Row 5: Sl 1, k5, p1, k2, p3, k2, sl 3.
Row 6: K3, p2, k3, p2, k1-tbl, p5, sssk.
Row 7: Sl 1, k5, p1, k2, p3, k2, sl 3.

Row 8: K3, p2, k1, k2tog, p2, k1-tbl, p5, sssk. 16 sts.
Row 9: Sl 1, k5, p1, k2, p2, k2, sl 3.
Row 10: K3, p2, k2tog, p2, k1-tbl, M1L, p5, sssk.
Row 11: Sl 1, k5, p2, k5, sl 3.
Row 12: K3, p5, k1-tbl, Left Leaf A, p3, sssk. 18 sts.
Row 13: Sl 1, k3, p3, k2, p1, k5, sl 3.
Row 14: K3, p5, k1-tbl, p2, k2, ssk, p2, sssk. 17 sts.
Row 15: Sl 1, k2, p3, kfb, k1, p1, k5, sl 3. 18 sts.
Row 16: K3, p5, k1-tbl, p3, ssk, k1, p2, sssk. 17 sts.
Row 17: Sl 1, k2, p2, k3, p1, k5, sl 3.
Row 18: K3, p5, M1R, k1-tbl, p3, ssk, p2, sssk.
Row 19: Sl 1, k6, p2, k5, sl 3.
Row 20: K3, p3, Right Leaf A, k1-tbl, p6, sssk. 19 sts.
Row 21: Sl 1, k6, p1, k2, p3, k3, sl 3.
Row 22: K3, p2, k2tog, {yo, k1} twice, p2, k1-tbl, p6, sssk. 20 sts.
Row 23: Sl 1, k6, p1, kfb, k1, p5, k2, sl 3. 21 sts.
Row 24: K3, p2, k5, p3, k1-tbl, p6, sssk.
Row 25: Sl 1, k6, p1, k3, p5, k2, sl 3.
Row 26: K3, p2, ssk, k1, k2tog, p3, k1-tbl, p6, sssk. 19 sts.
Row 27: Sl 1, k6, p1, k3, p3, k2, sl 3.
Row 28: K3, p2, k3tog, p3, k1-tbl, p6, sssk. 17 sts.
Row 29: Sl 1, k6, p1, k6, sl 3.
Row 30: K3, p6, k1-tbl, M1L, p6, sssk. 18 sts.
Row 31: Sl 1, k6, p2, k6, sl 3.
Row 32: K3, p6, k1-tbl, Left Leaf A, p4, sssk. 20 sts.
Row 33: Sl 1, k4, p3, k2, p1, k6, sl 3.
Row 34: K3, p6, k1-tbl, p2, {k1, yo} twice, ssk, p3, sssk. 21 sts.
Row 35: Sl 1, k3, p5, kfb, k1, p1, k6, sl 3. 22 sts.
Row 36: K3, p6, k1-tbl, p3, k4, ssk, p2, sssk. 21 sts.
Row 37: Sl 1, k2, p5, k3, p1, k6, sl 3.
Row 38: K3, p6, k1-tbl, p3, ssk, k1, k2tog, p2, sssk.
Row 39: Sl 1, k2, p3, k3, p1, k6, sl 3.
Row 40: K3, p6, k1-tbl, p3, sssk, p2, sssk.
Row 41: Sl 1, k6, p1, k6, sl 3.
Row 42: K3, p6, M1R, k1-tbl, p6, sssk.
Row 43: Sl 1, k6, p2, k6, sl 3.
Row 44: K3, p4, Right Leaf A, k1-tbl, p6, sssk.
Row 45: Sl 1, k6, p1, k2, p3, k4, sl 3.
Row 46: K3, p3, k2tog, {yo, k1} twice, p2, k1-tbl, p6, sssk.
Row 47: Sl 1, k6, p1, kfb, k1, p5, k3, sl 3.
Row 48: K3, p2, k2tog, k4, p3, k1-tbl, p6, sssk.
Row 49: Sl 1, k6, p1, k3, p5, k2, sl 3.
Row 50: K3, p2, ssk, k1, k2tog, p3, k1-tbl, p6, sssk.
Row 51: Sl 1, k6, p1, k3, p3, k2, sl 3.
Row 52: K3, p2, k3tog, p3, k1-tbl, p6, sssk.
Row 53: Sl 1, k6, p1, k6, sl 3.
Row 54: K3, p6, Inc-3, p6, sssk.
Row 55: Sl 1, k6, p3, k6, sl 3.

Row 56: K3, p6, {k1, yo} twice, ssk, p5, sssk.
Row 57: Sl 1, k5, p5, k6, sl 3.
Row 58: K3, p6, k2, {yo, k1} twice, ssk, p4, sssk.
Row 59: Sl 1, k4, p7, k6, sl 3.
Row 60: K3, p6, ssk, k3, k2tog, p4, sssk.
Row 61: Sl 1, k4, p5, k6, sl 3.
Row 62: K3, p6, ssk, k1, k2tog, p4, sssk.
Row 63: Sl 1, k4, p3, k6, sl 3.
Row 64: K3, p6, sssk, p4, sssk.

19

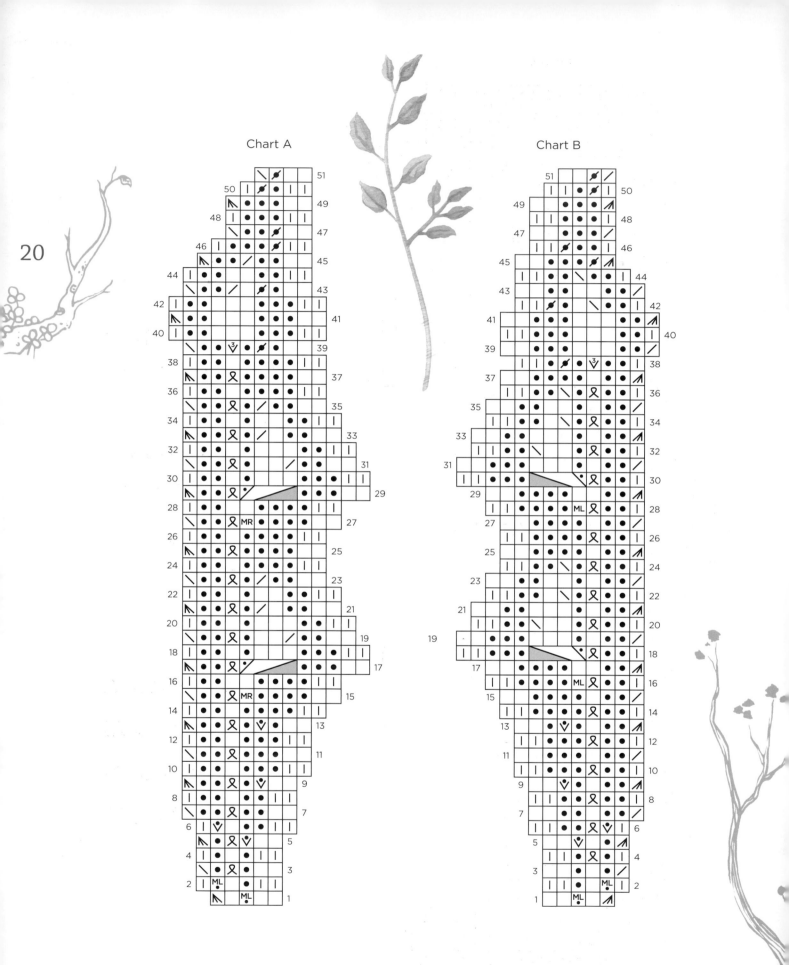

Chart A

Chart B

20

Chart C

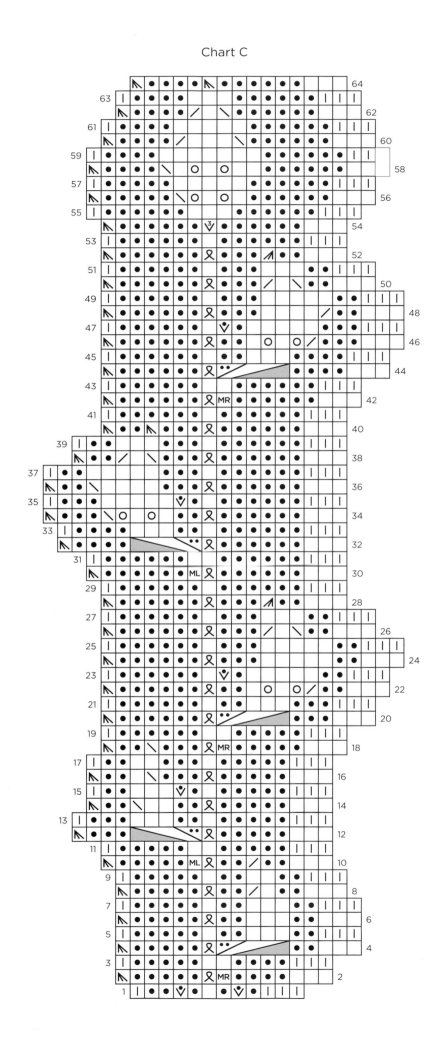

Legend:

☐	knit RS rows, purl WS rows
•	purl RS rows, knit WS rows
ℛ	k1-tbl
I	sl purlwise with yarn in back on RS sl purlwise with yarn in front on WS
/	k2tog on RS, p2tog on WS
\	ssk
⋉	sssk
⋌	k3tog on RS, p3tog on WS
⋎	p2tog on RS, k2tog on WS
O	yo
V	pfb on RS, kfb on WS
V³	Inc-3
ML	M1L
MR	M1R
ML•	M1-p

Left Leaf A: Sl 1 to cn, hold to front, p2 from left needle, Inc -3 from cn.

Right Leaf A: Sl 2 to cn, hold to back, Inc-3 from left needle, p2 from cn.

Left Leaf B: Sl 1 to cn, hold to front, p1 from left needle, Inc -3 from cn.

Right Leaf B: Sl 1 to cn, hold to back, Inc-3 from left needle, p1 from cn.

Flourish

A flourishing vine climbs up the left front of this otherwise classic cardigan.
Watch the vine grow as you knit the sweater pieces from the bottom up
and seam them together at the end.

{ FINISHED MEASUREMENTS }

Chest: 34¾ (38, 41, 44¼, 47½)[50¾, 54, 57, 60¼]" /
88 (96.5, 104.5, 112.5, 120.5)[129, 137, 145, 153] cm
Length: 21½ (22¼, 23, 23¾, 24½)[25¼, 26¼, 27, 28]" /
54.5 (56.5, 58, 60, 62)[64, 66.5, 68.5, 71] cm
Shown in size 34¾" / 88 cm
To be worn with 1–3" / 2.5–7.5 cm of positive ease.

{ MATERIALS }

5 (6, 6, 7, 7)[8, 8, 9, 10] skeins Juniper Moon Farm *Moonshine*
[40% Wool, 40% Alpaca, 20% Silk; 197 yd / 180 m
per 3½ oz / 100 g skein] in #0012 Rope Swing
OR approx 925 (1025, 1125, 1225, 1325)[1450, 1550,
1675, 1825] yd / 850 (925, 1025, 1125, 1225)[1325, 1425,
1525, 1675] m of a worsted weight wool or wool blend

Alternate Yarn: The Fibre Company *Organik*

US7 / 4.5 mm 32" / 80 cm circular needle
and 3 double-pointed needles for three-needle bind off
US6 / 4 mm 32" / 80 cm circular needle

Stitch markers, cable needle, stitch holders, tapestry needle
6 (6, 6, 6, 7)[7, 7, 7, 8] buttons 1¼"/ 3 cm diameter

{ GAUGE }

20 sts and 26 rows over 4" / 10 cm in St st
on US7 / 4.5 mm needles
Or size needed for accurate gauge.

Back

CO 86 (94, 102, 110, 118)[126, 134, 142, 150] sts
onto larger circular needle.

Ribbing set up row (WS): P2, {k2, p2}, rep.

Work even in est rib patt until piece measures 2" / 5 cm from CO
edge. End with a WS row. Change to St st as follows:

Dec row (RS): K2, ssk, knit until 4 sts rem, k2tog, k2. 2 sts dec.

Rep dec row when piece measures 3" / 7.5 cm and 4" / 10 cm. 80 (88,
96, 104, 112)[120, 128, 136, 144] sts.

Work even until piece measures 6" / 15 cm from CO edge. End with a
WS row.

Inc row (RS): K2, M1R, knit until 2 sts rem, M1L, k2. 2 sts inc.

Rep inc row when piece measures 8" / 20.5 cm from CO edge. 84 (92,
100, 108, 116)[124, 132, 140, 148] sts.

Work even until piece measures 13½ (13¾, 14¼, 14½, 15)[15¼, 15¾,

16, 16½]" / 34.5 (35, 36, 37, 38)[38.5, 40, 40.5, 42] cm from CO
edge. End with a RS row.

ARMHOLE SHAPING

BO 5 (6, 7, 8, 9)[10, 11, 12, 13] sts at beg of next 2 rows.

Dec row (RS): K2, ssk, knit until 4 sts rem, k2tog, k2. 2 sts dec.

Rep dec row every RS row 2 (4, 6, 7, 9)[11, 12, 14, 15] times more. 68
(70, 72, 76, 78)[80, 84, 86, 90] sts.

Work even until armhole measures 7 (7½, 7¾, 8¼, 8½)[9, 9½, 10,
10½]" / 18 (19, 19.5, 21, 21.5)[23, 24, 25.5, 26.5] cm. End with
a WS row.

SHOULDER SHAPING

Short Row 1 (RS): Knit until 6 (6, 7, 7, 7)[7, 8, 8, 8] sts rem, w&t.
Short Row 2 (WS): Purl until 6 (6, 7, 7, 7)[7, 8, 8, 8] sts rem, w&t.
Short Row 3 (RS): Knit until 6 (6, 7, 7, 7)[7, 8, 8, 8] sts rem before
last wrapped st, w&t.
Short Row 4 (WS): Purl until 6 (6, 7, 7, 7)[7, 8, 8, 8] sts rem before
last wrapped st, w&t.

Next row (RS): Knit across row picking up and knitting wraps as
you go.
Next row (WS): Purl across row picking up and purling wraps as
you go.

Next row (RS): K18 (19, 20, 21, 21)[22, 23, 24, 25] shoulder sts, BO
until 17 (18, 19, 20, 20)[21, 22, 23, 24] sts rem, knit to end. 18 (19,
20, 21, 21)[22, 23, 24, 25] sts rem for each shoulder.

Cut yarn leaving a long tail. Slide shoulder sts onto 2 separate holders
to be worked later.

Left Front

CO 42 (46, 50, 54, 58)[62, 66, 70, 74] sts onto larger circular needle.

Ribbing set up row (WS): P2, {k2, p2}, rep to end.

Work even in est rib patt until piece measures 2" / 5 cm from CO edge.
End with a WS row. Establish St st, Rev St st and Chart as follows:

Dec row (RS): K7 (11, 15, 19, 23)[27, 31, 35, 39], k2tog, k1, pm, p4,
pm, begin Chart over 17 sts, pm, p9, k2. 41 (45, 49, 53, 57)[61, 65,
69, 73] sts.

Work even in est patt until piece measures 3" / 7.5 cm from CO edge.
End with a WS row.

Dec row (RS): Knit to 3 sts before marker, k2tog, k1, p4, work
Chart, p9, k2. 1 st dec.

Work even in est patt until piece measures 4" / 10 cm from CO edge.

End with a WS row.

Rep dec row once more. 39 (43, 47, 51, 55)[59, 63, 67, 71] sts.

Work even in est patt until piece measures 6" / 15 cm from CO edge. End with a WS row.

Inc row (RS): Knit to 2 sts before marker, M1R, k2, p4, work Chart, p9, k2. 1 st inc.

Work even in est patt until piece measures 8" / 20.5 cm from CO edge. End with a WS row.

Rep inc row once more. 41 (45, 49, 53, 57)[61, 65, 69, 73] sts.

Once Chart has been completed, remove marker and work sts as they appear.

AT THE SAME TIME, work even in est patt until piece measures 13½ (13¾, 14¼, 14½, 15)[15¼, 15¾, 16, 16½]" / 34.5 (35, 36, 37, 38) [38.5, 40, 40.5, 42] cm from CO edge. End with a WS row.

ARMHOLE SHAPING
BO 5 (6, 7, 8, 9)[10, 11, 12, 13] sts at beg of next row.

Work 1 WS row even.

Dec row (RS): K3, ssk, work even until end. 1 st dec.

Rep dec row every RS row 2 (4, 6, 7, 9)[11, 12, 14, 15] times more.

When armhole measures 4 (4¼, 4½, 4¾, 5)[5¼, 5½, 5¾, 6]" / 10 (11, 11.5, 12, 12.5)[13.5, 14, 14.5, 15] cm, shape neckline as follows:

BO 9 sts at beg of next WS row.

Dec row (RS): Work even across row until 3 sts rem, p2tog, k1. 1 st dec.

Rep dec row every RS row 5 (5, 5, 6, 7)[7, 8, 8, 9] times more. 18 (19, 20, 21, 21)[22, 23, 24, 25] sts.

Work even until armhole opening measures 7 (7½, 7¾, 8¼, 8½)[9, 9½, 10, 10½]" / 18 (19, 19.5, 21, 21.5)[23, 24, 25.5, 26.5] cm. End with a RS row.

SHOULDER SHAPING
Short Row 1 (WS): Work across row in patt until 6 (6, 7, 7, 7)[7, 8, 8, 8] sts rem, w&t.
Short Row 2 (RS): Work to end.
Short Row 3 (WS): Work across row in patt until 6 (6, 7, 7, 7)[7, 8, 8, 8] sts rem before last wrapped st, w&t.
Short Row 4 (RS): Work to end.

Next row (WS): Work across row in patt, picking up and working wraps as you go.

Cut yarn. Slide shoulder sts onto a stitch holder to be worked later.

Right Front

CO 42 (46, 50, 54, 58)[62, 66, 70, 74] sts onto larger circular needle.

Ribbing set up row (WS): P2, {k2, p2}, rep.

Work even in est rib patt until piece measures 2" / 5 cm from CO edge. End with a RS row. Establish St st and Rev St st as follows:

Dec row (RS): K2, p30, k1, ssk, k7 (11, 15, 19, 23)[27, 31, 35, 39]. 41 (45, 49, 53, 57)[61, 65, 69, 73] sts.

Work even in est patt until piece measures 3" / 7.5 cm from CO edge. End with a WS row.

Dec row (RS): K2, p30, k1, ssk, knit to end. 1 st dec.

Work even in est patt until piece measures 4" / 10 cm from CO edge. End with a WS row.

Rep dec row once more. 39 (43, 47, 51, 55)[59, 63, 67, 71] sts.

Work even in est patt until piece measures 6" / 15 cm from CO edge. End with a WS row.

Inc row (RS): K2, p30, k2, M1L, knit to end. 1 st inc.

Work even in est patt until piece measures 8" / 20.5 cm from CO edge. End with a WS row.

Rep inc row once more. 41 (45, 49, 53, 57)[61, 65, 69, 73] sts.

Work even in est patt until piece measures 13½ (13¾, 14¼, 14½, 15) [15¼, 15¾, 16, 16½]" / 34.5 (35, 36, 37, 38)[38.5, 40, 40.5, 42] cm from CO edge. End with a RS row.

ARMHOLE SHAPING
BO 5 (6, 7, 8, 9)[10, 11, 12, 13] sts at beg of next WS row.

Dec row (RS): Work even in est patt until 5 sts rem, k2tog, k3. 1 st dec.

Rep dec row every RS row 2 (4, 6, 7, 9)[11, 12, 14, 15] times more. 33 (34, 35, 37, 38)[39, 41, 42, 44] sts.

When armhole measures 4 (4¼, 4½, 4¾, 5)[5¼, 5½, 5¾, 6]" / 10 (11, 11.5, 12, 12.5)[13.5, 14, 14.5, 15] cm, shape neckline as follows:

BO 9 sts at beg of next RS row.

Next row (WS): Work even to last st, p1.

Dec row (RS): K1, p2tog, work even to end. 1 st dec.

Rep dec row every RS row 5 (5, 5, 6, 7)[7, 8, 8, 9] times more. 18 (19, 20, 21, 21)[22, 23, 24, 25] sts.

Work even until armhole measures 7 (7½, 7¾, 8¼, 8½)[9, 9½, 10, 10½]" / 18 (19, 19.5, 21, 21.5)[23, 24, 25.5, 26.5] cm. End with a WS row.

SHOULDER SHAPING

Short Row 1 (RS): Work across row in patt until 6 (6, 7, 7, 7)[7, 8, 8, 8] sts rem, w&t.

Short Row 2 (WS): Work to end.

Short Row 3 (RS): Work across row in patt until 6 (6, 7, 7, 7)[7, 8, 8, 8] sts rem before last wrapped st, w&t.

Short Row 4 (WS): Work to end.

Next row (RS): Work across row in patt, picking up and working wraps sts as you go.

Work 1 WS row even.

Cut yarn. Slide shoulder sts onto a stitch holder to be worked later.

Sleeves (MAKE 2)

CO 42 (42, 46, 46, 50)[50, 54, 54, 58] sts onto larger circular needle.

Ribbing set up row (WS): P2, {k2, p2}, rep.

Work even in est rib patt until piece measures 2" / 5 cm from CO edge. End with a WS row. Change to St st and begin inc as follows:

Inc row (RS): K2, M1R, knit until 2 sts rem, M1L, k2. 2 sts inc.

Rep inc row every 14 (8, 8, 6, 6)[4, 4, 4, 4] rows 4 (1, 1, 4, 4)[1, 1, 7, 10] time(s) more, then every 16 (10, 10, 8, 8)[6, 6, 6, 6] rows 2 (8, 8, 8, 8)[14, 14, 10, 8] times more. 56 (62, 66, 72, 76)[82, 86, 90, 96] sts.

Work even until piece measures 17" / 43 cm from CO edge. End with a WS row.

SLEEVE CAP SHAPING

BO 5 (6, 7, 8, 9)[10, 11, 12, 13] sts at beg of next 2 rows.

Dec row (RS): K2, ssk, work even until 4 sts rem, k2tog, k2. 2 sts dec.

Rep dec row every RS row 2 (4, 6, 7, 9)[11, 12, 14, 15] times, then every 4th row 4 (3, 2, 2, 2)[2, 2, 3, 3] times, then every RS row 6 (7, 7, 8, 7)[7, 7, 5, 6] times. 20 sts.

Purl 1 WS row.

BO 2 sts at beg of next 2 rows, then 3 sts at beg of next 2 rows. BO rem 10 sts. Cut yarn.

Finishing

Return shoulder sts to spare dpns and seam shoulders together using three-needle bind off method.

NECKBAND

With smaller circular needle and RS facing, beg at the right side of the neck opening and pick up and knit 28 (30, 32, 33, 34)[36, 37, 39, 40] sts along right front, 32 (32, 32, 34, 36)[36, 38, 38, 40] from back neck, and 28 (30, 32, 33, 34)[36, 37, 39, 40] sts along left front. 88 (92, 96, 100, 104)[108, 112, 116, 120] sts.

Next row (WS): Knit all sts tbl.

Knit 3 rows. End with a RS row.

Next row (WS): BO all sts knitwise. Cut yarn.

BUTTON BAND

With smaller circular needle and RS facing, beg at the left front neck edge and pick up and knit 88 (92, 92, 96, 100)[104, 108, 108, 112] sts along left front edge.

Ribbing set up row (WS): P3, {k2, p2}, rep until 1 st rem, p1.

Cont in est rib patt for 10 rows more. End with a WS row.

Next row (RS): BO all sts in rib. Cut yarn.

BUTTONHOLE BAND

With smaller circular needle and RS facing, beg at the bottom CO edge of the right front and pick up and knit 88 (92, 92, 96, 100)[104, 108, 108, 112] sts along right front edge.

Ribbing set up row (WS): P3, {k2, p2}, rep until 1 st rem, p1.

Cont in est rib patt for 4 rows more. End with a WS row.

Buttonhole row (RS): Work 5 sts in patt, BO 3, {work 11 (11, 12, 13, 11)[11, 12, 13, 12] sts in patt, BO 3} 1 (1, 1, 1, 2)[2, 2, 2, 1] time(s), {work 11 (12, 13, 13, 11)[12, 13, 13, 11] sts in patt, BO 3, work 11 (12, 12, 13, 11)[12, 12, 13, 11] sts in patt, BO 3} 2 (2, 2, 2, 2)[2, 2, 2, 3] times, work in patt to end.

Next row (WS): Work across row in est rib patt. Using backwards loop method, CO 3 sts over each BO space.

Cont in est rib patt for 4 rows more. End with a WS row.

Next row (RS): BO all sts in patt. Cut yarn.

Set in sleeves and sew up side and arm seams. Weave in all ends on the WS. Wet block to measurements. Sew on buttons opposite buttonholes.

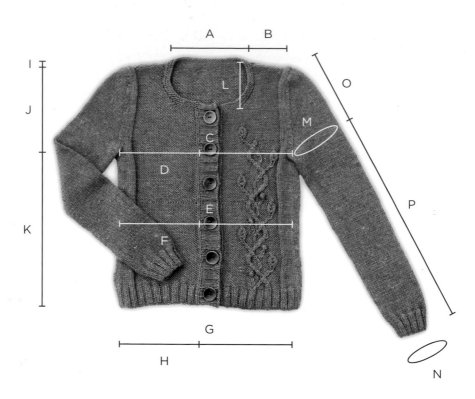

A	Back neck width	6½ (6½, 6½, 6¾, 7¼)[7¼, 7½, 7½, 8]" 16.5 (16.5, 16.5, 17.5, 18.5)[18.5, 19.5, 19.5, 20.5] cm
B	Shoulder width	3½ (3¾, 4, 4¼, 4¼)[4½, 4½, 4¾, 5]" 9 (9.5, 10, 10.5, 10.5)[11, 11.5, 12, 12.5] cm
C	Back chest width	16¾ (18½, 20, 21½, 23¼)[24¾, 26½, 28, 29½]" 42.5 (46.5, 51, 55, 59)[63, 67, 71, 75] cm
D	Front chest width*	8¼ (9, 9¾, 10½, 11½)[12¼, 13, 13¾, 14½]" 21 (23, 25, 27, 29)[31, 33, 35, 37] cm
E	Back waist width	16 (17½, 19¼, 20¾, 22½)[24, 25½, 27¼, 28¾]" 40.5 (44.5, 49, 53, 57)[61, 65, 69, 73] cm
F	Front waist width*	7¾ (8½, 9½, 10¼, 11)[11¾, 12½, 13½, 14¼]" 20 (22, 24, 26, 28)[30, 32, 34, 36] cm
G	Back hip width	17¼ (18¾, 20½, 22, 23½)[25¼, 26¾, 28½, 30]" 43.5 (48, 52, 56, 60)[64, 68, 72, 76] cm
H	Front hip width*	8½ (9¼, 10, 10¾, 11½)[12½, 13¼, 14, 14¾]" 21.5 (23.5, 25.5, 27.5, 29.5)[31.5, 33.5, 35.5, 37.5] cm
I	Shoulder height	½" / 1.5 cm
J	Armhole depth	7¼ (7¾, 8, 8½, 8¾)[9¼, 9¾, 10¼, 10¾]" 18.5 (20, 20.5, 21.5, 22.5)[23.5, 25, 26, 27.5] cm
K	Side length	13½ (13¾, 14¼, 14½, 15)[15¼, 15¾, 16, 16½]" 34.5 (35, 36, 37, 38)[38.5, 40, 40.5, 42] cm
L	Neck depth	3¼ (3½, 3½, 3¾, 3¾)[4, 4¼, 4½, 4¾]" 8.5 (9, 9, 9.5, 9.5)[10.5, 11, 11.5, 12] cm
M	Upper arm circ	11¼ (12½, 13¼, 14½, 15¼)[16½, 17¼, 18, 19¼]" 28.5 (31.5, 33.5, 36.5, 38.5)[41.5, 43.5, 45.5, 49] cm
N	Cuff circ	8½ (8½, 9¼, 9¼, 10)[10, 10¾, 10¾, 11½]" 21.5 (21.5, 23.5, 23.5, 25.5)[25.5, 27.5, 27.5, 29.5] cm
O	Cap height	6¼ (6½, 6½, 7, 7½)[8, 8¼, 9, 9½]" 15.5 (16.5, 16.5, 18, 19)[20.5, 21, 22.5, 24] cm
P	Sleeve length	17" / 43 cm

* measurement does not include button band

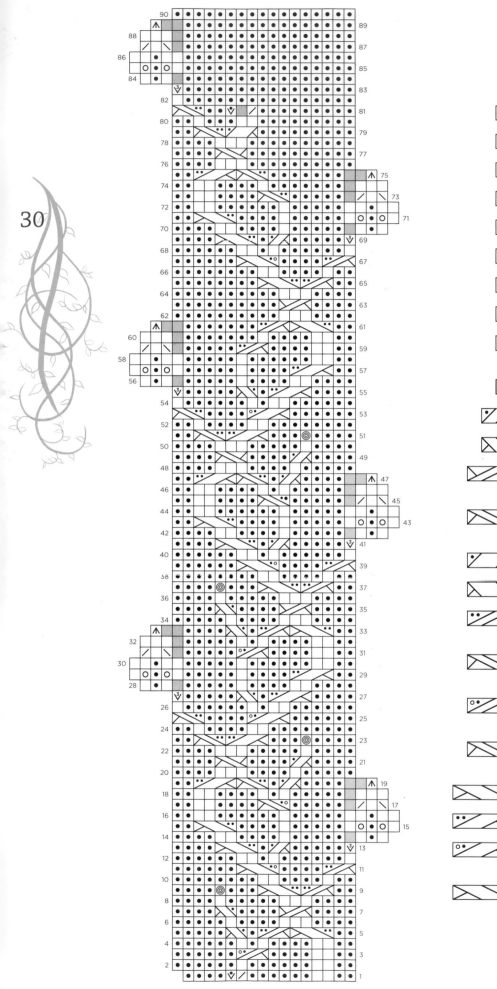

Chart

□	knit RS rows, purl WS rows
•	purl RS rows, knit WS rows
O	yo
pfb	pfb
M3	M3
/	k2tog
\	ssk
⋀	S2KP2
◎	MB: Make Bobble. M3, turn. K3, turn. P3 then slip 2nd and 3rd st over the 1st st and off the needle. K1-tbl.
▨	no stitch
T2B	T2B: Twist 2 Back
T2F	T2F: Twist 2 Front
C3BR	C3BR: Cable 3 Back Right. Sl 2 sts to cn and hold to back. K1 from left needle, then k2 from cn.
C3FL	C3FL: Cable 3 Front Left. Sl 1 st to cn and hold to front. K2 from left needle, then k1 from cn.
T3B	T3B: Twist 3 Back
T3F	T3F: Twist 3 Front
T3BR	T3BR: Twist 3 Back Right. Sl 2 sts to cn and hold to back. K1 from left needle, then p2 from cn.
T3FL	T3FL: Twist 3 Front Left. Sl 1 st to cn and hold to front. P2 from left needle, then k1 from cn.
T3BR-pk	T3BR-pk: Twist 3 Back Right, Purl, Knit. Sl 2 sts to cn and hold to back. K1 from left needle, then p1, k1 from cn.
T3FL-kp	T3FL-kp: Twist 3 Front Left, Knit, Purl. Sl 1 st to cn and hold to front. K1, p1 from left needle, then k1 from cn.
T4F	T4F: Twist 4 Front
T4B	T4B: Twist 4 Back
T4B-pk	T4B-pk: Twist 4 Back, Purl, Knit. Sl 2 sts to cn and hold to back. K2 from left needle, then p1, k1 from cn.
T4F-kp	T4F-kp: Twist 4 Front, Knit, Purl. Sl 2 sts to cn and hold to front. K1, p1 from left needle, then k2 from cn.

30

Chart

Row 1 (RS): P2, k2, p6, k2tog, pfb, p4.

Row 2 (WS): K6, p1, k6, p2, k2.

Row 3: P2, k2, p4, T3BR-pk, p6.

Row 4: K6, p1, k1, p1, k4, p2, k2.

Row 5: P2, T4F, T3BR, p1, T2F, p5.

Row 6: K5, p1, k4, p3, k4.

Row 7: P4, C3BR, p4, T2F, p4.

Row 8: K4, p1, k5, p3, k4.

Row 9: P2, T3BR, T4F, p3, MB, p4.

Row 10: K8, p2, k4, p1, k2.

Row 11: T3BR, p4, T4F-kp, p6.

Row 12: K6, p2, k1, p1, k6, p1.

Row 13: M3, p5, T2B, p1, T4F, p4. 19 sts.

Row 14: K4, p2, k4, p1, k5, p1, k1, p1.

Row 15: K1, yo, p1, yo, k1, p5, k1, p4, T4F, p2. 21 sts.

Row 16: K2, p2, k6, p1, k5, p2, k1, p2.

Row 17: Ssk, k1, k2tog, p5, T3FL-kp, p4, k2, p2. 19 sts.

Row 18: K2, p2, k4, p1, k1, p1, k5, p3.

Row 19: S2KP2, p4, T2B, p1, T3FL, T4B, p2. 17 sts.

Row 20: K4, p3, k4, p1, k5.

Row 21: P4, T2B, p4, C3FL, p4.

Row 22: K4, p3, k5, p1, k4.

Row 23: P4, MB, p3, T4B, T3FL, p2.

Row 24: K2, p1, k4, p2, k8.

Row 25: P6, T4B-pk, p4, T3FL.

Row 26: P1, k6, p1, k1, p2, k6.

Row 27: P4, T4B, p1, T2F, p5, M3. 19 sts.

Row 28: P1, k1, p1, k5, p1, k4, p2, k4.

Row 29: P2, T4B, p4, k1, p5, k1, yo, p1, yo, k1. 21 sts.

Row 30: P2, k1, p2, k5, p1, k6, p2, k2.

Row 31: P2, k2, p4, T3BR-pk, p5, ssk, k1, k2tog. 19 sts.

Row 32: P3, k5, p1, k1, p1, k4, p2, k2.

Row 33: P2, T4F, T3BR, p1, T2F, p4, S2KP2. 17 sts.

Row 34: K5, p1, k4, p3, k4.

Rows 35–62: As for rows 7–34.

Row 63: P4, C3BR, p10.

Row 64: K10, p3, k4.

Row 65: P2, T3BR, T4F, p8.

Row 66: K8, p2, k4, p1, k2.

Row 67: T3BR, p4, T4F-kp, p6,

Row 68: K6, p2, k1, p1, k6, p1.

Row 69: M3, p5, T2B, p1, T4F, p4. 19 sts.

Row 70: K4, p2, k4, p1, k5, p1, k1, p1.

Row 71: K1, yo, p1, yo, k1, p5, k1, p4, T4F, p2. 21 sts.

Row 72: K2, p2, k6, p1, k5, p2, k1, p2.

Row 73: Ssk, k1, k2tog, p5, T3FL, p4, k2, p2.

Row 74: K2, p2, k4, p1, k7, p3.

Row 75: S2KP2, p7, T3FL, T4B, p2.

Row 76: K4, p3, k10.

Row 77: P10, C3FL, p4.

Row 78: K4, p3, k10.

Row 79: P9, T3B, T3FL, p2.

Row 80: K2, p1, k3, p2, k9.

Row 81: P9, k2tog, pfb, p2, T3FL.

Row 82: P1, k16.

Row 83: P16, M3. 19 sts.

Row 84: P1, k1, p1, k16.

Row 85: P16, k1, yo, p1, yo, k1. 21 sts.

Row 86: P2, k1, p2, k16.

Row 87: P16, ssk, k1, k2tog. 19 sts.

Row 88: P3, k16.

Row 89: P16, S2KP2. 17 sts.

Row 90: Knit.

bare branches

This cozy sweater-coat features an A-line skirt, rounded back hemline, romantic oversized hood and secret tree motif only visible when the hood is worn. *Bare Branches* is worked in pieces from the bottom up and seamed together at the end.

{ FINISHED MEASUREMENTS }

Chest: 34 (38, 42, 46)[50, 54, 58, 62]" /
86.5 (96.5, 106.5, 117)[127, 137, 147.5, 157.5] cm
Length: 26¼ (27¼, 28¼, 29¼)[30¼, 31¼, 32¼, 33¼]" /
67 (69.5, 72, 74.5)[77, 79.5, 82, 84.5] cm
Shown in size 34" / 86.5 cm
To be worn with 2–3" / 5–7.5 cm of positive ease.

{ MATERIALS }

13 (15, 16, 17)[18, 20, 21, 23] skeins Rowan *Felted Tweed Aran*
[50% Wool, 25% Alpaca, 25% Viscose; 95 yd / 87 m
per 1¾ oz / 50 g skein] in #720 OR approx 1225 (1350,
1475, 1575)[1700, 1875, 2000, 2125] yd / 1125 (1225, 1350,
1450)[1575, 1725, 1825, 1950] m of an aran weight wool
or wool blend

Alternate Yarn: Jamieson's *Aran*

US8 / 5 mm 32" / 80 cm circular needle
and 3 double-pointed needles for three-needle bind off

Stitch holders, stitch markers in different colors,
cable needle, tapestry needle,
3 buttons 1" / 2.5 cm diameter,
sewing needle and matching thread

{ GAUGE }

16 sts and 23 rows over 4" / 10 cm in St st
on US8 / 5 mm needles
Or size needed for accurate gauge.

Back

CO 90 (98, 106, 114)[122, 130, 138, 146] sts.

Purl 1 WS row.

Cont in St st for 6 rows more. End with a WS row. Create a folded hem as follows:

Knit each st of next row together with the loops of the CO edge.

Purl 1 WS row.

Short Row 1 (RS): Knit until 10 sts rem, w&t.
Short Row 2 (WS): Purl until 10 sts rem, w&t.
Short Row 3 (RS): Knit until 10 sts rem from last wrapped st, w&t.
Short Row 4 (WS): Purl until 10 sts rem from last wrapped st, w&t.

Rep short rows 3 and 4 once more. 6 wrapped sts.

Next row (RS): Knit across row picking up and knitting wraps as you go.

Next row (WS): Purl across row picking up and purling wraps as you go.

Work even in St st until piece measures 2" / 5 cm from bottom of hem in the shortest section.

End with a WS row.

Dec row (RS): K2, ssk, knit until 4 sts rem, k2tog, k2. 2 sts dec.

Rep dec row every 12th row 5 times more. 78 (86, 94, 102)[110, 118, 126, 134] sts.

Work even in St st until piece measures 15 (15½, 15½, 16)[16, 16½, 16½, 17]" / 38 (39.5, 39.4, 40.5)[40.5, 42, 42, 43] cm from bottom of hem. End with a WS row.

Dec row (RS): K31 (35, 39, 43)[47, 51, 55, 59], ssk twice, sssk, k2, k3tog, k2tog twice, k31 (35, 39, 43)[47, 51, 55, 59]. 70 (78, 86, 94)[102, 110, 118, 126] sts.

Purl 1 WS row.

BODICE

Begin working Chart in between markers with Rev St st on either side.

Set up row (RS): P16 (20, 24, 28)[32, 36, 40, 44], pm, work Chart over 35 sts, pm, p19 (23, 27, 31)[35, 39, 43, 47].

AT THE SAME TIME, work until bodice measures 4 (4, 4½, 4½)[5, 5, 5½, 5½]" / 10 (10, 11.5, 11.5)[12.5, 12.5, 14, 14] cm. End with a WS row.

ARMHOLE SHAPING

BO 3 (4, 4, 5)[5, 6, 7, 8] sts at beg of next 2 rows.

Next row (RS): P1, p2tog, purl to marker, sm, work Chart, sm, purl until 3 sts rem, p2tog, p1. 2 sts dec.

Rep dec row every RS row 0 (2, 5, 7)[10, 12, 14, 16] times more. 62 (64, 66, 68)[70, 72, 74, 76] sts.

Work even in est patt, working all sts in Rev St st once rows 1–50 of Chart are complete, until armhole measures 6¾ (7¼, 7¾, 8¼)[8¾, 9¼, 9¾, 10¼]" / 17 (18.5, 19.5, 21)[22, 23.5, 25, 26] cm. End with a WS row.

SHOULDER SHAPING

Short Row 1 (RS): Purl until 5 (5, 5, 6)[6, 6, 6, 6] sts rem, w&t.
Short Row 2 (WS): Knit until 5 (5, 5, 6)[6, 6, 6, 6] sts rem, w&t.
Short Row 3 (RS): Purl until 5 (5, 5, 6)[6, 6, 6, 6] sts rem from last wrapped st, w&t.
Short Row 4 (WS): Knit until 5 (5, 5, 6)[6, 6, 6, 6] sts rem from last wrapped st, w&t.

Next row (RS): Purl across row picking up and purling wraps as you go.

Next row (WS): Knit across row picking up and knitting wraps as you go.

Next row: P15 (16, 16, 17)[17, 18, 18, 19], BO 32 (32, 34, 34)[36, 36, 38, 38] sts purlwise, p14 (15, 15, 16)[16, 17, 17, 18]. Cut yarn.

Slide unworked shoulder sts onto 2 separate holders to be worked later. 15 (16, 16, 17)[17, 18, 18, 19] sts rem for each shoulder.

Left Front
CO 47 (51, 55, 59)[63, 67, 71, 75] sts.

Purl 1 WS row.

Cont in St st for 6 rows more. End with a WS row. Create a folded hem as follows:

Knit each st of next row together with the loops of the CO edge.

Purl 1 WS row.

Work even in St st until piece measures 2" / 5 cm from bottom of hem. End with a WS row.

Dec row (RS): K2, ssk, knit to end. 1 st dec.

Rep dec row every 12 rows 5 times more. 41 (45, 49, 53)[57, 61, 65, 69] sts.

Work even in St st until piece measures 15 (15½, 15½, 16)[16, 16½, 16½, 17]" / 38 (39.5, 39.5, 40.5)[40.5, 42, 42, 43] from bottom of hem. End with a WS row.

Dec row (RS): K18 (21, 24, 27)[30, 33, 36, 39], k3tog, k2, k3tog, k15 (16, 17, 18)[19, 20, 21, 22]. 37 (41, 45, 49)[53, 57, 61, 65] sts.

Purl 1 WS row.

BODICE
Switch to Rev St st and work I-cord border as follows:

Next row (RS): Purl to last 3 sts, sl 3 purlwise with yarn in back.
Next row (WS): P3 loosely, knit to end.

NOTE: Slipping last 3 sts of every row maintains the I-cord border. It may be helpful to work the first 3 sts more loosely than normal on the subsequent row to avoid the fabric pulling too tight.

Work even as est until bodice measures 4 (4, 4½, 4½)[5, 5, 5½, 5½]" / 10 (10, 11.5, 11.5)[12.5, 12.5, 14, 14] cm. End with a WS row.

ARMHOLE SHAPING
Next row (RS): BO 3 (4, 4, 5)[5, 6, 7, 8], cont in est patt to end.

Work 1 WS row.

Next row: P1, p2tog, work even to end. 1 st dec.

Rep dec row every RS row 0 (2, 5, 7)[10, 12, 14, 16] times more. 33 (34, 35, 36)[37, 38, 39, 40] sts.

Work even in est patt until armhole measures 6¾ (7¼, 7¾, 8¼)[8¾, 9¼, 9¾, 10¼)" / 17 (18.5, 19.5, 21)[22, 23.5, 25, 26] cm. End with a RS row.

SHOULDER SHAPING
Short Row 1 (WS): Knit until 5 (5, 5, 6)[6, 6, 6, 6] sts rem, w&t.
Short Row 2 (RS): Purl to end.
Short Row 3 (WS): Knit until 5 (5, 5, 6)[6, 6, 6, 6] sts rem from last wrapped st, w&t.
Short Row 4 (RS): Purl to end.

Next row (WS): Work even across row picking up and knitting wraps as you go.

Work 1 RS row.

With WS facing, slide first 18 (18, 19, 19)[20, 20, 21, 21] sts onto a stitch holder for the hood. Slide rem 15 (16, 16, 17)[17, 18, 18, 19] sts on a second stitch holder for the shoulder. Cut yarn.

Right Front
CO 47 (51, 55, 59)[63, 67, 71, 75] sts.

Purl 1 WS row.

Cont in St st for 6 rows more. End with a WS row. Create a folded hem as follows:

Knit each st of next row tog with the loops of the CO edge.

Purl 1 WS row.

Work even in St st until piece measures 2" / 5 cm from bottom of hem. End with a WS row.

Dec row (RS): Knit until 4 sts rem, k2tog, k2. 1 st dec.

Rep dec row every 12 rows 5 times more. 41 (45, 49, 53)[57, 61, 65, 69] sts.

Work even in St st until piece measures 15 (15½, 15½, 16)[16, 16½, 16½, 17]" / 38 (39.5, 39.5, 40.5)[40.5, 42, 42, 43] cm from bottom of hem. End with a WS row.

Dec row (RS): K15 (16, 17, 18)[19, 20, 21, 22], k3tog-tbl, k2, k3tog-tbl, k18 (21, 24, 27)[30, 33, 36, 39]. 37 (41, 45, 49)[53, 57, 61, 65] sts.

Purl 1 WS row.

BODICE
Switch to Rev St st and work I-cord border, beginning with a Button-loop row, as follows:

Button-loop row (RS): {K3, sl 3 sts back to left needle} 3 times, k3, purl to end.

Next row (WS): Knit until 3 sts rem, sl 3 sts purlwise with yarn in front.
Next row (RS): K3 loosely, purl to end.

Rep button-loop row on a RS row every 2 (2, 2¼, 2¼)[2½, 2½, 2¾, 2¾]" / 5 (5, 5.5, 5.5)[6, 6, 7, 7] cm twice more.

Bodice measures approx 4 (4, 4½, 4½)[5, 5, 5½, 5½]" / 10 (10, 11.5, 11.5)[12.5, 12.5, 14, 14] cm. End with a RS row.

ARMHOLE SHAPING
Next row (WS): BO 3 (4, 4, 5)[5, 6, 7, 8], cont in est patt to end.
Next row (RS): Work even until 3 sts rem, p2tog, k1. 1 st dec.

Rep dec row every RS row 0 (2, 5, 7)[10, 12, 14, 16] times more. 33 (34, 35, 36)[37, 38, 39, 40] sts.

Work even in est patt until armhole measures 6¾ (7¼, 7¾, 8¼)[8¾, 9¼, 9¾, 10¼]" / 17 (18.5, 19.5, 21)[22, 23.5, 25, 26] cm. End with a WS row.

SHOULDER SHAPING

Short Row 1 (RS): Purl until 5 (5, 5, 6)[6, 6, 6, 6] sts rem, w&t.
Short Row 2 (WS): Knit to end.
Short Row 3 (RS): Purl until 5 (5, 5, 6)[6, 6, 6, 6] sts rem from last wrapped st, w&t.
Short Row 4 (WS): Knit to end.

Next row (RS): Work even across row picking up and purling wraps as you go.

Work 1 WS row. Turn, k3, slide sts back to left needle.

With RS facing, slide first 18 (18, 19, 19)[20, 20, 21, 21] sts onto a stitch holder for the hood. Slide rem 15 (16, 16, 17)[17, 18, 18, 19] sts on a second stitch holder for the shoulder. Cut yarn.

Sleeves (MAKE 2)

CO 38 (38, 38, 38)[38, 42, 42, 42] sts.

Purl 1 WS row.

Cont in St st for 6 rows more. End with a WS row. Create a folded hem as follows:

Knit each st of next row together with the loops of the CO edge.

Purl 1 WS row.

Work even in St st until piece measures 2" / 5 cm from bottom of hem. End with a WS row.

Inc row (RS): K2, M1R, knit to last 2 sts, M1L, k2. 2 sts inc.

Rep inc row every 16 (10, 8, 6)[6, 4, 4, 4] rows 5 (2, 5, 4)[12, 5, 11, 17] times more, then every - (12, 10, 8)[8, 6, 6, 6] rows 0 (5, 4, 7)[1, 10, 6, 2] time(s) more. 50 (54, 58, 62)[66, 74, 78, 82] sts.

Work even in St st until sleeve measures 17" / 43 cm from bottom of hem. End with a WS row.

SLEEVE CAP SHAPING

BO 3 (4, 4, 5)[5, 6, 7, 8] sts at beg of next 2 rows.

Dec row (RS): K2, ssk, knit until 4 sts rem, k2tog, k2. 2 sts dec.

Rep dec row every RS row 12 (13, 15, 16)[18, 20, 21, 22] times more. 18 (18, 18, 18)[18, 20, 20, 20] sts.

Purl 1 WS row.

BO 3 sts at beg of next 2 rows. BO rem 12 (12, 12, 12)[12, 14, 14, 14] sts. Cut yarn.

Hood

Return shoulder sts to spare dpns, and seam shoulders together using three-needle bind off method.

Return 18 (18, 19, 19)[20, 20, 21, 21] right front hood sts to circular needle. Sl 3, add yarn and knit across. Pick up and knit 43 (43, 45, 45)[47, 47, 49, 49] sts along BO edge of back neck. Return left front hood sts to spare needle and knit until 3 sts rem, sl 3 purlwise with yarn in back. 79 (79, 83, 83)[87, 87, 91, 91] sts.

Set up row (WS): P8, pfb, p18 (18, 20, 20)[22, 22, 24, 24], pfb, p10, pm, p3, pm, p10, pfb, p18 (18, 20, 20)[22, 22, 24, 24], pfb, p5, sl 3. 83 (83, 87, 87)[91, 91, 95, 95] sts.

Next row (RS): Knit until 3 sts rem, sl 3 purlwise with yarn in back.
Next row (WS): Purl until 3 sts rem, sl 3 purlwise with yarn in front.

Work even as est until piece measures 9½" / 24 cm from beg of hood. End with a WS row.

Dec row (RS): Knit until 2 sts rem before first marker, k2tog, sm, k3, sm, ssk, knit until 3 sts rem, sl 3. 2 sts dec.

Rep dec row every 4 rows 4 times more, then every RS row once more. 71 (71, 75, 75)[79, 79, 83, 83] sts.

Next row (WS): Removing markers as you go, knit to marker, k2tog, knit to end of row. 70 (70, 74, 74)[78, 78, 82, 82] sts.

Divide rem sts in half and slide onto two separate dpns. 35 (35, 37, 37)[39, 39, 41, 41] sts on each needle.

Graft sts together using the kitchener st. Cut yarn.

Finishing

Set in sleeves and sew up side and arm seams. Weave in all ends on the WS. Wet block to measurements. Sew on buttons opposite buttonholes.

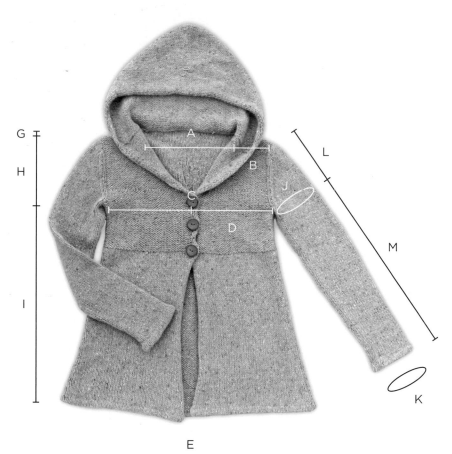

A	Back neck width	8 (8, 8½, 8½)[9, 9, 9½, 9½]"
		20.5 (20.5, 21.5, 21.5)[23, 23, 24, 24] cm
B	Shoulder width	3¾ (4, 4, 4¼)[4¼, 4½, 4½, 4¾]"
		9.5 (10, 10, 11)[11, 11.5, 11.5, 12] cm
C	Back chest width	17½ (19½, 21½, 23½)[25½, 27½, 29½, 31½]"
		44.5 (49.5, 54.5, 59.5)[65, 60, 75, 80] cm
D	Front chest width	8¾ (9¾, 10¾, 11¾)[12¾, 13¾, 14¾, 15¾]"
		22 (25, 27.5, 30)[32.5, 35, 37.5, 40] cm
E	Back hem width	22½ (24½, 26½, 28½)[30½, 32½, 34½, 36½]"
		57 (62, 67.5, 72.5)[77.5, 82.5, 87.5, 92.5] cm
F	Front hem width	11¾ (12¾, 13¾, 14¾)[15¾, 16¾, 17¾, 18¾]"
		30 (32.5, 35, 37.5)[40, 42.5, 45, 47.5] cm
G	Shoulder height	¾" / 2 cm
H	Armhole depth	7 (7½, 8, 8½)[9, 9½, 10, 10½]"
		18 (19.5, 20.5, 22)[23, 24.5, 25.5, 27] cm
I	Side length	19¼ (19¾, 20¼, 20¾)[21¼, 21¾, 22¼, 22¾]"
		49 (50.5, 51.5, 53)[54, 55.5, 57, 58] cm
J	Upper arm circ	12½ (13½, 14½, 15½)[16½, 18½, 19½, 20½]"
		32 (34.5, 37, 39.5)[42, 47, 49.5, 52] cm
K	Cuff circ	9½ (9½, 9½, 9½)[9½, 10½, 10½, 10½]"
		24 (24, 24, 24)[24, 26.5, 26.5, 26.5] cm
L	Cap height	5¼ (5½, 6¼, 6½)[7¼, 8, 8¼, 8¾]"
		13.5 (14, 16, 17)[18.5, 20.5, 21, 22] cm
M	Sleeve length	17" / 43 cm

40

	knit RS rows, purl WS rows			T2B: Twist 2 Back			T3FL: Twist 3 Front Left. Sl 1 st to cn and hold to front. P2 from left needle, then k1 from cn.
•	purl RS rows, knit WS rows			T2F: Twist 2 Front			
	p2tog			T3B: Twist 3 Back			T4B: Twist 4 Back
ML	M1L			T3F: Twist 3 Front			T4F: Twist 4 Front
MR	M1R						

Chart (WORKED OVER 35 STS)

Rows 1, 3, 5, 7 (RS): P17, k4, p14.

Rows 2, 4, 6, 8 (WS): K14, p4, k17.

Row 9: P15, p2tog, M1R, k4, p14.

Row 10: K14, p5, k16.

Row 11: P14, p2tog, k1, M1R, k4, p14.

Row 12: K14, p6, k15.

Row 13: P13, T4B, k4, p14.

Row 14: K14, p4, k2, p2, k13.

Row 15: P11, T4B, p2, k4, p14.

Row 16: K14, p4, k4, p2, k11.

Row 17: P9, T4B, p4, k2, T4F, p12.

Row 18: K12, p2, k2, p2, k6, p2, k9.

Row 19: P7, T4B, p4, p2tog, M1R, k2, p2, T4F, p10.

Row 20: K10, p2, k4, p3, k7, p2, k7.

Row 21: P5, T4B, p5, p2tog, k1, M1R, k2, p4, T4F, p8.

Row 22: K8, p2, k6, p4, k8, p2, k5.

Row 23: P4, T3B, p6, T4B, k2, M1L, p2tog, p4, T4F, p6.

Row 24: K6, p2, k7, p3, k2, p2, k7, p2, k4.

Row 25: P3, T3B, p6, T3B, p2, k2, M1L, k1, p2tog, p5, T4F, p4.

Row 26: K4, p2, k8, p4, k3, p2, k7, p2, k3.

Row 27: P2, T2B, T2F, p5, T3B, p3, k2, T4F, p6, k1, T3FL, p2.

Row 28: K2, p1, k2, p1, k6, p2, k2, p2, k4, p2, k5, p1, k2, p1, k2.

Row 29: P1, T2B, p2, k1, p4, T3B, p4, k2, p2, T3F, p5, k1, p2, T2F, p1.

Row 30: K1, p1, k3, p1, k5, p2, k3, p2, k5, p2, k4, p1, k3, p1, k1.

Row 31: T2B, p1, p2tog, M1R, k1, p4, k2, p5, k2, p3, k1, T2F, p8, k1, p1.

Row 32: K1, p1, k8, p1, k1, p1, k3, p2, k5, p2, k4, p2, k3, p1.

Row 33: P3, T2B, T2F, p2, T2B, k1, p3, p2tog, M1R, k2, p3, k1, p1, T2F, p5, p2tog, M1R, k1, p1.

Row 34: K1, p2, k6, p1, k2, p1, k3, p3, k4, p1, k1, p1, k2, p1, k2, p1, k3.

Row 35: P3, k1, p4, T2B, p1, k1, M1L, p2tog, p1, T3B, k1, p6, k1, M1L, p2tog, p4, k1, T2F.

Row 36: P1, k1, p1, k5, p2, k6, p1, k1, p2, k2, p2, k2, p1, k4, p1, k3.

Row 37: P10, T2B, k1, p1, T3B, p1, T2F, p4, T2B, T2F, p3, T2B, p2.

Row 38: K3, p1, k3, p1, k2, p1, k4, p1, k3, p2, k1, p1, k1, p1, k10.

Row 39: P12, k1, p1, k2, p3, T2F, p3, k1, p6, k1, p3.

Row 40: K3, p1, k6, p1, k3, p1, k4, p2, k1, p1, k12.

Row 41: P12, k1, p1, k1, T2F, p3, T2F, p2, k1, p5, T2B, p3.

Row 42: K4, p1, k5, p1, k2, p1, k4, p1, k1, p1, k1, p1, k12.

Row 43: P14, k1, p1, T2F, p3, k1, p2, k1, p10.

Row 44: K13, p1, k3, p1, k2, p1, k14.

Row 45: P14, k1, p2, k1, M1L, p2tog, p15.

Row 46: K16, p2, k2, p1, k14.

Row 47: P13, T2B, p1, T2B, T2F, p15.

Row 48: K15, p1, k2, p1, k2, p1, k13.

Row 49: P16, k1, p18.

Row 50: K18, p1, k16.

sunlit autumn

A lightweight cardigan with lovely autumn leaf lace insets
on the upper back and pockets, along with A-line shaping in the back
to flatter your waistline. *Sunlit Autumn* is knit in pieces from the bottom up
and seamed together at the end.

{ FINISHED MEASUREMENTS }

Chest: 31¾ (35½, 39¼, 42¾, 46½)[50, 53¾, 57¼, 61]" /
81 (90, 99.5, 108.5, 118)[127, 136.5, 145.5, 155] cm
Length: 21¾ (22¾, 23¾, 24¼, 25¼)[26¼, 26¾, 27¾, 28¾]" /
55.5 (58, 60.5, 61.5, 64.5)[67, 68, 70.5, 73] cm
Shown in size 31¾" / 81 cm
To be worn with 0–2"/ 0–5 cm of positive ease.

{ MATERIALS }

5 (5, 6, 6, 7)[8, 8, 9, 9] skeins Sunshine Yarns *Merino Sport*
[100% Superwash Merino Wool; 225 yd / 205 m
per 3½ oz / 100 g skein] in Pumpkin
OR approx 975 (1075, 1200, 1300, 1450) [1600, 1700,
1825, 1950] yd / 875 (1000, 1100, 1200, 1300)[1450, 1550,
1675, 1775] m of a sport weight wool or wool blend

Alternate Yarn: Cascade Yarns *220 Sport*

US5 / 3.75 mm 32" / 80 cm circular needle
and 3 double-pointed needles for three-needle bind off
US4 / 3.5 mm 60" / 150 cm circular needle

Stitch markers, cable needle, stitch holders,
tapestry needle, 3 hook and eye closures,
sewing needle and matching thread

{ GAUGE }

22 sts and 30 rows over 4" / 10 cm in St st
on US5 / 3.75 mm needles
Or size needed for accurate gauge.

Pocket Linings (MAKE 2)

CO 27 sts onto larger circular needle.

Purl 1 row.

Work even in St st until piece measures 4" / 10 cm. End with a WS row.

BO 2 sts, k22 sts, BO last 2 sts. Cut yarn. Place rem 23 live sts onto stitch holder to be used later.

Back

CO 97 (107, 117, 127, 137)[147, 157, 167, 177] sts onto larger circular needle.

Knit 9 rows.

Purl 1 WS row.

Work even in St st until piece measures 3" / 7.5 cm from CO edge. End with a RS row.

Set up row (WS): P33 (38, 43, 48, 53)[58, 63, 68, 73], pm, p31, pm, p33 (38, 43, 48, 53)[58, 63, 68, 73].

Dec row (RS): Knit until 2 sts rem before marker, ssk, knit to next marker, k2tog, knit to end. 2 sts dec.

Rep dec row every 18 rows 3 times more. Remove markers. 89 (99, 109, 119, 129)[139, 149, 159, 169] sts.

Work even in St st until piece measures 14½ (15, 15½, 15¾, 16¼) [16¾, 17, 17½, 18]" / 37 (38, 39.5, 40, 41.5)[42.5, 43, 44.5, 45.5] cm from CO edge. End with a WS row, placing markers as follows on last WS row: P30 (35, 40, 45, 50)[55, 60, 65, 70], pm, p29, pm, p30 (35, 40, 45, 50)[55, 60, 65, 70].

ARMHOLE SHAPING

BO 3 (4, 5, 6, 7)[8, 9, 10, 11] sts at beg of next 2 rows, then 0 (0, 0, 0, 2)[2, 3, 3, 3] sts at beg of next 0 (0, 0, 0, 2)[4, 4, 6, 8] rows.

Dec row (RS): K2, ssk, work across row in patt until 4 sts rem, k2tog, k2. 2 sts dec.

Rep dec row every RS row 0 (3, 6, 8, 9)[10, 10, 10, 11] times. 81 (83, 85, 89, 91)[93, 97, 99, 99] sts.

AT THE SAME TIME, when piece measures 15½ (16, 16½, 16¾, 17¼) [17¾, 18, 18½, 19]" / 39.5 (40.5, 42, 42.5, 44)[45, 45.5, 47, 48.5] cm from CO edge, begin working Chart A between markers. When chart is finished, remove markers and work even in St st.

Work even until armhole measures 6½ (7, 7½, 7¾, 8¼)[8¾, 9, 9½, 10]" / 16.5 (18, 19, 19.5, 21)[22, 23, 24, 25.5] cm. End with a WS row.

SHOULDER SHAPING

Short Row 1 (RS): Knit until 6 (7, 7, 7, 8)[8, 8, 9, 9] sts rem, w&t.
Short Row 2 (WS): Purl until 6 (7, 7, 7, 8)[8, 8, 9, 9] sts rem, w&t.
Short Row 3 (RS): Knit until 6 (7, 7, 7, 8)[8, 8, 9, 9] sts rem before last wrapped st, w&t.
Short Row 4 (WS): Purl until 6 (7, 7, 7, 8)[8, 8, 9, 9] sts rem from last wrapped st, w&t.

Next row (RS): Knit across row, picking up and knitting wraps as you go.
Next row (WS): Purl across row, picking up and purling wraps as you go.

Next row (RS): K19 (20, 21, 22, 23)[24, 25, 26, 26] shoulder sts, BO until 18 (19, 20, 21, 22) [23, 24, 25, 25] sts rem, knit to end. 19 (20, 21, 22, 23)[24, 25, 26, 26] sts rem for each shoulder.

Cut yarn leaving a long tail. Slide unworked shoulder sts onto 2 separate holders to be worked later.

Left Front

CO 39 (44, 49, 54, 59)[64, 69, 74, 79] sts onto larger circular needle.

Knit 9 rows.

Next row (WS): P5, pm, p23, pm, purl to end of row.

Work even in St st until piece measures 2½" / 6.5 cm from CO edge. End with a WS row.

Next row (RS): Knit to marker, work Chart B over 23 sts, k5.

Cont in est patt through chart row 21, then cont in St st for 3 rows more. End with a WS row.

POCKET BORDER

Row 1 (RS): Knit to marker, p23, k5.
Row 2 (WS): Purl.

Rep last 2 rows twice more.

JOIN POCKET LINING

Next row (RS): Knit to marker. With a separate ball of yarn, BO next 23 pocket sts purlwise, cut yarn. With original strand of yarn, k23 pocket lining sts from stitch holder, knit to end. Remove markers.

Work even in St st until piece measures 14½ (15, 15½, 15¾, 16¼)[16¾, 17, 17½, 18]" / 37 (38, 39.5, 40, 41.5)[42.5, 43, 44.5, 45.5] cm from CO edge. End with a WS row.

ARMHOLE SHAPING

BO 3 (4, 5, 6, 7)[8, 9, 10, 11] sts at beg of next row, then 0 (0, 0, 0, 2)[2, 3, 3, 3] sts at beg of next 0 (0, 0, 0, 1)[2, 2, 3, 4] RS row(s).

Purl 1 WS row.

Dec row (RS): K2, ssk, work to end. 1 st dec.

Rep dec row every RS row 0 (3, 6, 8, 9)[10, 10, 10, 11] times.

AT THE SAME TIME, when piece measures 15 (15½, 16, 16¼, 16¾)[17¼, 17½, 18, 18½]" / 38 (39.5, 40.5, 41.5, 42.5)[44, 44.5, 45.5, 47] cm from CO edge, shape neckline as follows:

Dec row (RS): Work until 4 sts rem, ssk, k2. 1 st dec.

Rep dec row every RS row 10 (9, 7, 8, 6)[5, 6, 5, 4] times more, then every 4th row 5 (6, 8, 8, 10)[11, 11, 12, 13] times more. 19 (20, 21, 22, 23)[24, 25, 26, 26] sts.

Work even until armhole measures 6½ (7, 7½, 7¾, 8¼)[8¾, 9, 9½, 10]" / 16.5 (18, 19, 19.5, 21)[22, 23, 24, 25.5] cm. End with a RS row.

SHOULDER SHAPING

Short Row 1 (WS): Purl until 6 (7, 7, 7, 8)[8, 8, 9, 9] sts rem, w&t.
Short Row 2 (RS): Knit to end.

Short Row 3 (WS): Purl until 6 (7, 7, 7, 8)[8, 8, 9, 9] sts rem before last wrapped st, w&t.
Short Row 4 (RS): Knit to end.

Next row (WS): Purl across row picking up and purling wraps as you go.

Cut yarn. Slide shoulder sts onto a stitch holder to be worked later.

Right Front

CO 39 (44, 49, 54, 59)[64, 69, 74, 79] sts onto larger circular needle.

Knit 9 rows. Purl 1 WS row.

Work even in St st until piece measures 2½" / 6.5 cm from CO edge. End with a WS row.

Next row (RS): K5, pm, work Chart B over 23 sts, pm, knit to end.

Cont in est patt through chart row 21, then cont in St st for 3 rows more. End with a WS row.

POCKET BORDER

Row 1 (RS): K5, p23, knit to end.
Row 2 (WS): Purl.

Rep last 2 rows twice more. Remove markers.

JOIN POCKET LINING

Next row (RS): K5. With a separate ball of yarn, BO next 23 pocket sts purlwise, cut yarn. With original strand of yarn, k23 pocket lining sts from stitch holder, knit to end.

Work even in St st until piece measures 14½ (15, 15½, 15¾, 16¼)[16¾, 17, 17½, 18]" / 37 (38, 39.5, 40, 41.5)[42.5, 43, 44.5, 45.5] cm from CO edge. End with a RS row.

ARMHOLE SHAPING

BO 3 (4, 5, 6, 7)[8, 9, 10, 11] sts at beg of next row, then 0 (0, 0, 0, 2)[2, 3, 3, 3] sts at beg of next 0 (0, 0, 0, 1)[2, 2, 3, 4] WS row(s).

Dec row (RS): Work until 4 sts rem, k2tog, k2. 1 st dec.

Rep dec row every RS row 0 (3, 6, 8, 9)[10, 10, 10, 11] times.

AT THE SAME TIME, when piece measures 15 (15½, 16, 16¼, 16¾)[17¼, 17½, 18, 18½]" / 38 (39.5, 40.5, 41.5, 42.5)[44, 44.5, 45.5, 47] cm from CO edge, shape neckline as follows:

Dec row (RS): K2, k2tog, work to end. 1 st dec.

Rep dec row every RS row 10 (9, 7, 8, 6)[5, 6, 5, 4] times, then every 4th row 5 (6, 8, 8, 10)[11, 11, 12, 13] times more. 19 (20, 21, 22, 23)[24, 25, 26, 26] sts.

Work even until armhole measures 6½ (7, 7½, 7¾, 8¼)[8¾, 9, 9½, 10]" / 16.5 (18, 19, 19.5, 21)[22, 23, 24, 25.5] cm. End with a WS row.

SHOULDER SHAPING

Short Row 1 (RS): Knit until 6 (7, 7, 7, 8)[8, 8, 9, 9] sts rem, w&t.

Short Row 2 (WS): Purl to end.

Short Row 3 (RS): Knit until 6 (7, 7, 7, 8)[8, 8, 9, 9] sts rem before last wrapped st, w&t.

Short Row 4 (WS): Purl to end.

Next row (RS): Knit across row picking up and knitting wraps as you go.

Cut yarn. Slide shoulder sts onto a stitch holder to be worked later.

Sleeves (MAKE 2)

CO 52 (54, 56, 58, 60)[64, 68, 72, 76] sts onto larger circular needle.

Knit 9 rows.

Purl 1 WS row.

Work even in St st until sleeve measures 2" / 5 cm from CO edge. End with a WS row.

Inc row (RS): K2, M1R, knit to last 2 sts, M1L, k2. 2 sts inc.

Rep inc row every 14 (12, 10, 8, 6)[6, 4, 4, 4] rows 3 (3, 2, 3, 7)[3, 14, 12, 10] times more, then every 0 (10, 8, 6, 4)[4, 2, 2, 2] rows 0 (2, 5, 6, 4)[10, 1, 5, 9] time(s) more. 60 (66, 72, 78, 84)[92, 100, 108, 116] sts.

Work even in St st until piece measures 11" / 28 cm from CO edge. End with a WS row.

SLEEVE CAP SHAPING

BO 3 (4, 5, 6, 7)[8, 9, 10, 11] sts at beg of next 2 rows, then 0 (0, 0, 0, 2)[2, 3, 3, 3] sts at beg of next 0 (0, 0, 0, 2)[4, 4, 6, 8] rows.

Dec row (RS): K2, ssk, knit until 4 sts rem, k2tog, k2. 2 sts dec.

Rep dec row every RS row 16 (18, 20, 22, 22)[23, 24, 24, 24] times more. 20 sts.

Purl 1 WS row.

BO 2 sts at beg of next 2 rows, then 3 sts at beg of next 2 rows. BO rem 10 sts. Cut yarn.

Finishing

Return shoulder sts to spare dpns and seam shoulders together using three-needle bind off method.

BANDS

With smaller circular needle and RS facing, beg at bottom CO edge of right front and pick up and knit 90 (93, 96, 97, 100)[103, 104, 107, 110] sts along right front edge to the beg of neckline shaping, pm, 38 (41, 44, 45, 48)[51, 52, 55, 58] sts along right front neckline edge, 43 (43, 43, 45, 45)[45, 47, 47, 47] sts along back neck, 38 (41, 44, 45, 48)[51, 52, 55, 58] sts along left front neckline edge to end of neckline shaping, pm, then 90 (93, 96, 97, 100)[103, 104, 107, 110] sts along left front edge. 299 (311, 323, 329, 341)[353, 359, 371, 383] sts.

Next row (WS): Knit to 1 st before marker, kfb, knit to next marker, kfb, knit to end.

Knit 5 rows. End with a RS row. Remove markers.

Next row (WS): BO all sts knitwise. Cut yarn.

Set in sleeves and sew up sleeve and side seams. Sew pocket linings to sweater body on the WS using the mattress st. Weave in all ends on the WS. Sew hook and eye closures to sweater fronts ½" / 1.5 cm apart starting the first closure right at the beginning of the neckline shaping. Wet block to measurements.

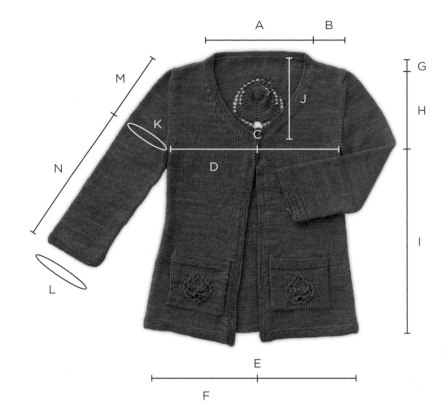

A	Back neck width	7¾ (7¾, 7¾, 8¼, 8¼)[8¼, 8½, 8½, 8½]" 20 (20, 20, 21, 21)[21, 21.5, 21.5, 21.5] cm
B	Shoulder width	3½ (3¾, 3¾, 4, 4¼)[4¼, 4½, 4¾, 4¾]" 9 (9.5, 9.5, 10, 11)[11, 11.5, 12, 12] cm
C	Back chest width	16¼ (18, 19¾, 21¾, 23½)[25¼, 27, 29, 30¾]" 41 (45.5, 50.5, 55, 59.5)[64, 69, 73.5, 78] cm
D, F	Front width* (chest, hip)	7 (8, 9, 9¾, 10¾)[11¾, 12½, 13½, 14¼]" 18 (20.5, 22.5, 25, 27)[29.5, 32, 34, 36.5] cm
E	Back hip width	17¾ (19½, 21¼, 23, 25)[26¾, 28½, 30¼, 32¼]" 45 (49.5, 54, 58.5, 63.5)[68, 72.5, 77, 81.5] cm
G	Shoulder height	½" / 1.5 cm
H	Armhole depth	6¾ (7¼, 7¾, 8, 8½)[9, 9¼, 9¾, 10¼]" 17 (18.5, 19.5, 20.5, 21.5)[23, 23.5, 25, 26] cm
I	Side length	14½ (15, 15½, 15¾, 16¼)[16¾, 17, 17½, 18]" 37 (38, 39.5, 40, 41.5)[42.5, 43, 44.5, 45.5] cm
J	Neck depth	6¾ (7¼, 7¾, 8, 8½)[9, 9¼, 9¾, 10¼]" 17.5 (18.5, 20, 20.5, 21.5)[23, 23.5, 25, 26] cm
K	Upper arm circ	11 (12, 13, 14¼, 15¼)[16¾, 18¼, 19¾, 21]" 27.5 (30.5, 33.5, 36, 39)[42.5, 46, 50, 53.5] cm
L	Cuff circ	9½ (9¾, 10¼, 10½, 11)[11¾, 12¼, 13, 13¾]" 24 (25, 26, 27, 27.5)[29.5, 31.5, 33.5, 35] cm
M	Cap height	5¼ (5¾, 6½, 7, 7¼)[7¾, 8, 8¼, 8½]" 13.5 (15, 16.5, 17.5, 18.5)[19.5, 20.5, 21, 21.5] cm
N	Sleeve length	11" / 28 cm

* measurement does not include button band

Chart A

Row 1 (RS): K14, Inc-3, k14. 31 sts.

Row 2 (WS): P13, p2tog-tbl, p1, p2tog, p13. 29 sts.

Row 3: K12, k2tog, yo, M5, yo, ssk, k12. 33 sts.

Row 4: P11, p2tog-tbl, p7, p2tog, p11. 31 sts.

Row 5: K10, S2KP2, yo, (k1, M1R) twice, k1, (M1L, k1) twice, yo, S2KP2, k10. 33 sts.

Row 6: P9, p2tog-tbl, p11, p2tog, p9. 31 sts.

Row 7: K8, S2KP2, yo, k1, M1R, k3, M1R, k1, M1L, k3, M1L, k1, yo, S2KP2, k8. 33 sts.

Row 8: P7, p2tog-tbl, p15, p2tog, p7. 31 sts.

Row 9: K6, S2KP2, yo, k1, M1R, k5, M1R, k1, M1L, k5, M1L, k1, yo, S2KP2, k6. 33 sts.

Row 10: P5, p2tog-tbl, p19, p2tog, p5. 31 sts.

Row 11: K4, S2KP2, yo, k1, M1R, k7, M1R, k1, M1L, k7, M1L, k1, yo, S2KP2, k4. 33 sts.

Row 12: P3, p2tog-tbl, p23, p2tog, p3. 31 sts.

Row 13: K2, S2KP2, yo, k1, M1R, k9, M1R, k1, M1L, k9, M1L, k1, yo, S2KP2, k2. 33 sts.

Row 14: P1, p2tog-tbl, p27, p2tog, p1. 31 sts.

Row 15: S2KP2, yo, ssk, k3, k2tog, yo, k1, M1R, k4, M1R, k1, M1L, k4, M1L, k1, yo, ssk, k3, k2tog, yo, S2KP2.

Rows 16, 18, 20 and 22: Purl.

Row 17: Ssk, yo, ssk, k1, k2tog, yo, k2tog, k6, M1R, k1, M1L, k6, ssk, yo, ssk, k1, k2tog, yo, k2tog.

Row 19: Ssk, yo, S2KP2, yo, k2tog, M1R, k7, M1R, k1, M1L, k7, M1L, ssk, yo, S2KP2, yo, k2tog.

Row 21: (Ssk, yo) twice, ssk, k3, k2tog, yo, k3, M1R, k1, M1L, k3, yo, ssk, k3, k2tog, (yo, k2tog) twice.

Row 23: M1R, k1, yo, S2KP2, yo, ssk, k1, k2tog, yo, k2tog, k7, ssk, yo, ssk, k1, k2tog, yo, S2KP2, yo, k1, M1L. 27 sts.

Row 24: P1, M1L, p25, M1R, p1. 29 sts.

Row 25: K2, M1R, k1, (yo, S2KP2) twice, yo, k2tog, k2, S2KP2, k2, ssk, yo, (S2KP2, yo) twice, k1, M1L, k2. 25 sts.

Row 26: P3, M1L, p19, M1R, p3. 27 sts.

Row 27: K4, M1R, k1, yo, S2KP2, (yo, ssk) twice, k3, (k2tog, yo) twice, S2KP2, yo, k1, M1L, k4.

Row 28: P5, M1L, p17, M1R, p5. 29 sts.

Row 29: K6, M1R, k1, yo, S2KP2, (yo, ssk) twice, k1, (k2tog, yo) twice, S2KP2, yo, k1, M1L, k6.

Row 30: P7, M1L, p15, M1R, p7. 31 sts.

Row 31: K8, M1R, k1, yo, S2KP2, yo, ssk, yo, S2KP2, yo, k2tog, yo, S2KP2, yo, k1, M1L, k8.

Row 32: P9, M1L, p13, M1R, p9. 33 sts.

Row 33: K10, M1R, k1, yo, S2KP2, yo, Dec 5, yo, S2KP2, yo, k1, M1L, k10. 31 sts.

Row 34: P11, M1L, p9, M1R, p11. 33 sts.

Row 35: K12, M1R, ssk, yo, Dec 5, yo, k2tog, M1L, k12. 31 sts.

Row 36: Purl.

Row 37: K13, M1R, Dec 5, M1L, k13. 29 sts.

Chart A

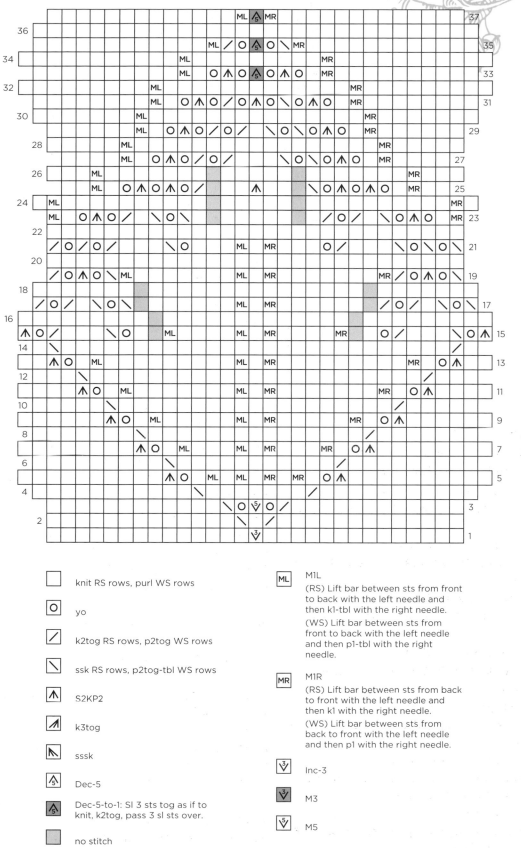

	knit RS rows, purl WS rows
O	yo
/	k2tog RS rows, p2tog WS rows
\	ssk RS rows, p2tog-tbl WS rows
⋀	S2KP2
⋀	k3tog
⋀	sssk
⋀	Dec-5
⋀	Dec-5-to-1: Sl 3 sts tog as if to knit, k2tog, pass 3 sl sts over.
	no stitch

ML	M1L (RS) Lift bar between sts from front to back with the left needle and then k1-tbl with the right needle. (WS) Lift bar between sts from front to back with the left needle and then p1-tbl with the right needle.
MR	M1R (RS) Lift bar between sts from back to front with the left needle and then k1 with the right needle. (WS) Lift bar between sts from back to front with the left needle and then p1 with the right needle.
V	Inc-3
V	M3
V	M5

49

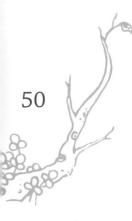

Chart B

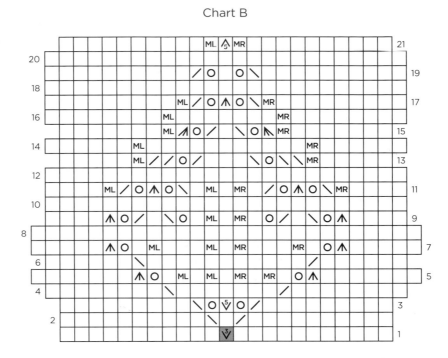

Chart B

Row 1 (RS): K11, M3, k11. 25 sts.

Row 2 (WS): P10, p2tog-tbl, p1, p2tog, p10. 23 sts.

Row 3: K9, k2tog, yo, M5, yo, ssk, k9. 27 sts.

Row 4: P8, p2tog-tbl, p7, p2tog, p8. 25 sts.

Row 5: K7, S2KP2, yo, (k1, M1R) twice, k1, (M1L, k1) twice, yo, S2KP2, k7. 27 sts.

Row 6: P6, p2tog-tbl, p11, p2tog, p6. 25 sts.

Row 7: K5, S2KP2, yo, k1, M1R, k3, M1R, k1, M1L, k3, M1L, k1, yo, S2KP2, k5. 27 sts.

Rows 8, 10 and 12: Purl.

Row 9: K4, S2KP2, yo, ssk, k1, k2tog, yo, k1, M1R, k1, M1L, k1, yo, ssk, k1, k2tog, yo, S2KP2, k4. 25 sts.

Row 11: K4, M1R, ssk, yo, S2KP2, yo, k2tog, k1, M1R, k1, M1L, k1, ssk, yo, S2KP2, yo, k2tog, M1L, k4.

Row 13: K5, M1R, ssk twice, yo, ssk, k3, k2tog, yo, k2tog twice, M1L, k5. 23 sts.

Row 14: P6, M1L, p11, M1R, p6. 25 sts.

Row 15: K7, M1R, sssk, yo, ssk, k1, k2tog, yo, k3tog, M1L, k7. 23 sts.

Row 16: P8, M1L, p7, M1R, p8. 25 sts.

Row 17: K9, M1R, ssk, yo, S2KP2, yo, k2tog, M1L, k9.

Rows 18 and 20: Purl.

Row 19: K10, ssk, yo, k1, yo, k2tog, k10.

Row 21: K10, M1R, Dec-5, M1L, k10. 23 sts.

ACCESSORIES

ferns

A slouchy-style hat with subtle fern stitch motifs
growing in two different directions.

Stretches to fit a 20–22" / 51–56 cm head circ

{ FINISHED MEASUREMENTS }
Brim circ: 18" / 46 cm unstretched

{ MATERIALS }
1 skein Berroco *Ultra Alpaca* [50% Wool,
50% Alpaca; 215 yd / 197 m per 3½ oz / 100 g skein]
in #6205 Dark Chocolate OR approx 125 yd / 110 m
of a worsted weight alpaca blend

Alternate Yarn: Cascade Yarns *Pure Alpaca*

US7 / 4.5 mm 16" / 40 cm circular needle
US9 / 5.5 mm 16" / 40 cm circular needle
and set of double-pointed needles

Stitch marker, cable needle, tapestry needle

{ GAUGE }
18 sts and 26 rows over 4" / 10 cm in St st
worked in the rnd on US9 / 5.5 mm needles
Or size needed for accurate gauge.

Brim

CO 100 sts onto smaller circular needle. Pm, join for working in the rnd being careful not to twist your sts.

Ribbing set up rnd: {K2, p2}, rep.

Work even in est rib patt for 1" / 2.5 cm.

Switch to larger circular needle.

Knit 1 rnd, move marker 2 sts to the left.

Work rnds 1–48 of Chart patt. Switch to dpns when work becomes too tight on the circular needle.

Finishing

Cut yarn, thread tail onto tapestry needle, pass through rem 5 live sts and cinch to close.

Weave in all ends on the WS.

Wet block.

Chart (WORKED 5 TIMES AROUND)

Rnd 1: {K4, C3BR, C3FL, k10}, rep.

All even rnds 2–34: Knit.

Rnd 3: {K2, C3BR, k4, C3FL, k8}, rep.

Rnd 5: {C3BR, k1, C3BR, C3FL, k1, C3FL, k6}, rep.

Rnd 7: {K2, C3BR, k4, C3FL, k8}, rep.

Rnd 9: {K1, C2B, k1, C3BR, C3FL, k1, C2F, k7}, rep.

Rnd 11: {K2, C3BR, k4, C3FL, k8}, rep.

Rnd 13: Move marker 2 sts to the left. {K2, C3BR, C3FL, k5, C2F, C2B, k3}, rep.

Rnd 15: {C3BR, k4, C3FL, k3, C2F, C2B, k3}, rep.

Rnd 17: {K2, C3BR, C3FL, k5, C2F, C2B, k3}, rep.

Rnd 19: {K1, C2B, k4, C2F, k4, C2F, C2B, k3}, rep.

Rnd 21: {K2, C3BR, C3FL, k4, C3FL, C3BR, k2}, rep.

Rnd 23: {K1, C2B, k4, C2F, k3, C3FL, C3BR, k2}, rep.

Rnd 25: {K2, C3BR, C3FL, k3, C2F, k4, C2B, k1}, rep.

Rnd 27: {K2, C3BR, C3FL, k4, C3FL, C3BR, k2}, rep.

Rnd 29: {K3, C2B, C2F, k4, C2F, k4, C2B, k1}, rep.

Rnd 31: {K3, C2B, C2F, k5, C3FL, C3BR, k2}, rep.

Rnd 33: {K3, C2B, C2F, k3, C3FL, k4, C3BR}, rep.

Rnd 35: {K3, C2B, C2F, k5, C3FL, C3BR, k2}, rep.

Rnd 36: {K12, k2tog, k2, ssk, k2}, rep. 90 sts.

Rnd 37: Move marker 1 st to the left. {K3, k2tog, k3, C3FL, k4, C3BR}, rep. 85 sts.

Rnd 38: Move marker 1 st to the left. {K6, k2tog, k6, ssk, k1}, rep. 75 sts.

Rnd 39: Move marker 1 st to the left. {K3, C2F, k1, C3FL, C3BR, k1, C2B}, rep.

Rnd 40: Move marker 1 st to the left. {K1, k2tog, k10, ssk}, rep. 65 sts.

Rnd 41: Move marker 1 st to the left. {K1, C3FL, k4, C3BR, k2}, rep.

Rnd 42: Move marker 1 st to the left. {K10, SK2P2}, rep. 55 sts.

Rnd 43: {K2, C3FL, C3BR, k3}, rep.

Rnd 44: Move marker 1 st to the left. {K8, S2KP2}, rep. 45 sts.

Rnd 45: Move marker 1 st to the left. {K6, S2KP2}, rep. 35 sts.

Rnd 46: Move marker 1 st to the left. {K4, S2KP2}, rep. 25 sts.

Rnd 47: Move marker 1 st to the left. {K2, S2KP2}, rep. 15 sts.

Rnd 48: Move marker 1 st to the left. S2KP2 5 times. 5 sts.

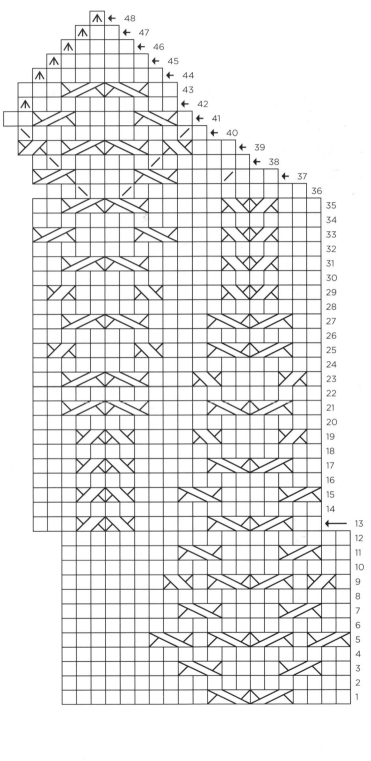

← 48
← 47
← 46
← 45
← 44
43
← 42
← 41
← 40
← 39
← 38
← 37
36
35
34
33
32
31
30
29
28
27
26
25
24
23
22
21
20
19
18
17
16
15
14
← 13
12
11
10
9
8
7
6
5
4
3
2
1

Chart

□	knit
╱	k2tog
╲	ssk
⋀	S2KP2
⧅	C2B: Cable 2 Back
⧄	C2F: Cable 2 Front
⧅	C3BR: Cable 3 Back Right. Sl 2 sts to cn and hold to back. K1 from left needle, then k2 from cn.
⧄	C3FL: Cable 3 Front Left. Sl 1 st to cn and hold to front. K2 from left needle, then k1 from cn.
←	Remove marker, sl 1 st from left needle to right needle, replace marker for new beg of rnd.
⟵	Remove marker, sl 2 sts from left needle to right needle, replace marker for new beg of rnd.

twigs and willows mitts

Lightweight, cropped fingerless mitts with a leafy branch gracefully extending over the back of the hand. Designed to coordinate with the *Twigs and Willows* cardigan from *Botanical Knits*.

{ SIZE }
Women's Medium

{ FINISHED MEASUREMENTS }
Width: approx 7" / 18 cm around at widest point of hand
Length: 7" / 18 cm

{ MATERIALS }
1 skein Brooklyn Tweed *Loft* [100% American Wool;
275 yd / 251 m per 1¾ oz / 50 g skein] in Fauna
OR approx 125 yd / 100 m of a fingering weight wool
or wool blend

Alternate Yarn: Jamieson's *Shetland Spindrift*

Set of US1 / 2.25 mm double-pointed needles
Set of US2 / 2.75 mm double-pointed needles

Stitch markers in 2 different colors,
cable needle, stitch holder, tapestry needle

{ GAUGE }
28 sts and 40 rows over 4" / 10 cm in St st
worked in the rnd on US2 / 2.75 mm needles
Or size needed for accurate gauge.

Cuff

With smaller needles, CO 48 sts onto 1 dpn. Divide sts evenly among 3 dpns. Pm, join for working in the rnd being careful not to twist your sts.

Ribbing set up rnd: {K2, p2}, rep.

Work even in est rib patt for 2" / 5 cm.

Switch to larger needles.

Hand

LEFT MITT ONLY

Rnd 1: K12, pm (contrasting color), work Rnd 1 of Chart A over 26 sts, pm (contrasting color), k10.
Rnds 2–4: Knit to marker, work chart as est to marker, knit to end.
Rnd 5: K9, M1R, k1, M1L, k2, work Rnd 5 of chart, knit to end. 52 sts.
Rnds 6, 8, 10, 12, 14, 16, 18, 20 and 22: Knit to marker, work chart as est to marker, knit to end.
Rnd 7: K9, M1R, k3, M1L, k2, work Rnd 7 of chart, knit to end. 56 sts.
Rnd 9: K9, M1R, k5, M1L, k2, work Rnd 9 of chart, knit to end. 58 sts.
Rnd 11: K9, M1R, k7, M1L, k2, work Rnd 11 of chart, knit to end. 60 sts.
Rnd 13: K9, M1R, k9, M1L, k2, work Rnd 13 of chart, knit to end. 62 sts.
Rnd 15: K9, M1R, k11, M1L, k2, work Rnd 15 of chart, knit to end. 64 sts.
Rnd 17: K9, M1R, k13, M1L, k2, work Rnd 17 of chart, knit to end. 66 sts.
Rnd 19: K9, M1R, k15, M1L, k2, work Rnd 19 of chart, knit to end. 68 sts.
Rnd 21: K9, slide next 17 sts onto stitch holder to be worked later, CO 1 st, k2, work Rnd 21 of chart, knit to end. 52 sts.
Rnds 23–38: Knit to marker, work chart as est to marker, knit to end. 50 sts after Rnd 29, 48 sts after Rnd 31.

RIGHT MITT ONLY

Remove marker, k2, pm for new beg of rnd.

Rnd 1: K10, pm (contrasting color), work Rnd 1 of Chart B over 26 sts, pm (contrasting color), k12.
Rnds 2–4: Knit to marker, work chart as est to marker, knit to end.
Rnd 5: K10, work Rnd 5 of chart, sm, k2, M1R, k1, M1L, k9. 52 sts.
Rnds 6, 8, 10, 12, 14, 16, 18, 20 and 22: Knit to marker, work chart as est to marker, knit to end.
Rnd 7: K10, work Rnd 7 of chart, k2, M1R, k3, M1L, k9. 56 sts.
Rnd 9: K10, work Rnd 9 of chart, k2, M1R, k5, M1L, k9. 58 sts.
Rnd 11: K10, work Rnd 11 of chart, k2, M1R, k7, M1L, k9. 60 sts.
Rnd 13: K10, work Rnd 13 of chart, k2, M1R, k9, M1L, k9. 62 sts.

Rnd 15: K10, work Rnd 15 of chart, k2, M1R, k11, M1L, k9. 64 sts.

Rnd 17: K10, work Rnd 17 of chart, k2, M1R, k13, M1L, k9. 66 sts.

Rnd 19: K10, work Rnd 19 of chart, k2, M1R, k15, M1L, k9. 68 sts.

Rnd 21: K10, work Rnd 21 of chart, k2, slide next 17 sts onto stitch holder to be worked later, CO 1 st, k9. 52 sts.

Rnds 23–38: Knit to marker, work chart as est to marker, knit to end. 50 sts after Rnd 29, 48 sts after Rnd 31.

BOTH MITTS

Remove contrasting color markers. Cont in est patt for 4 rnds more.

Knit 1 rnd.

Purl 1 rnd.

Rep last 2 rnds once more.

Knit 1 rnd.

BO purlwise. Remove marker. Cut yarn.

Thumb

Return 17 held sts to dpns and divide evenly among 3 needles. Rejoin yarn.

Rnd 1: K17, pick up and knit 1 st on left side of thumb opening, 1 middle st in previous CO, and 1 more st on right side of thumb opening. Pm to mark the beg of rnd. 20 sts.

Rnd 2: K17, k3-tbl.

Cont in St st for 3 rnds more.

Purl 1 rnd.

Knit 1 rnd.

Rep last 2 rnds once more.

BO purlwise. Remove marker.

Finishing

Cut yarn. Weave in all ends on the WS. Wet block.

	knit RS rows, purl WS rows	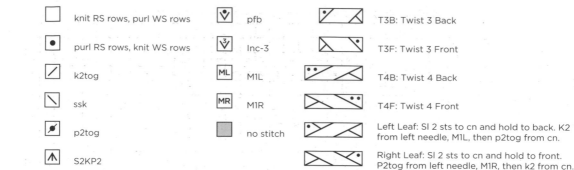	pfb		T3B: Twist 3 Back
•	purl RS rows, knit WS rows	³∨	Inc-3		T3F: Twist 3 Front
╱	k2tog	ML	M1L		T4B: Twist 4 Back
╲	ssk	MR	M1R		T4F: Twist 4 Front
⊠	p2tog		no stitch		Left Leaf: Sl 2 sts to cn and hold to back. K2 from left needle, M1L, then p2tog from cn.
⋀	S2KP2				Right Leaf: Sl 2 sts to cn and hold to front. P2tog from left needle, M1R, then k2 from cn.

64

Chart A

Rnd 1: T4F, k2, {p2, k2} 5 times.

Rnd 2: P2, k4, {p2, k2} 5 times.

Rnd 3: P2, Right Leaf, {p2, k2} 5 times.

Rnd 4: P3, k3, {p2, k2} 5 times.

Rnd 5: P3, Inc-3, T4F, k2, {p2, k2} 4 times. 28 sts.

Rnd 6: P3, k1, p1, k1, p2, k4, {p2, k2} 4 times.

Rnd 7: P2, pfb, k1, M1R, p1, M1L, ssk, p1, T3F, k1, {p2, k2} 4 times. 30 sts.

Rnd 8: P4, k2, p1, k2, p2, k3, {p2, k2} 4 times.

Rnd 9: P3, pfb, k2, p1, k1, ssk, p1, Right Leaf, p1, k2, {p2, k2} 3 times.

Rnd 10: P5, k5, p2, k3, p1, k2, {p2, k2} 3 times.

Rnd 11: P5, ssk, k1, k2tog, p2, Inc-3, T4F, k1, {p2, k2} 3 times.

Rnd 12: P5, k3, p2, k1, p1, k1, p2, k3, {p2, k2} 3 times.

Rnd 13: P5, S2KP2, p1, pfb, k1, M1R, p1, M1L, ssk, p1, T3F, {p2, k2} 3 times.

Rnd 14: P9, k2, p1, k2, {p2, k2} 4 times.

Rnd 15: P8, pfb, k2, p1, k1, ssk, p1, Right Leaf, k2, {k2, p2} twice.

Rnd 16: P10, k5, p2, k5, {p2, k2} twice.

Rnd 17: P10, ssk, k1, k2tog, p2, Inc-3, T4F, {p2, k2} twice.

Rnd 18: P10, k3, p2, k1, p1, k1, {p2, k2} 3 times.

Rnd 19: P10, S2KP2, p1, pfb, k1, M1R, p1, M1L, ssk, p1, T3F, p1, k2, p2, k2.

Rnd 20: P14, {k2, p1, k2, p2} twice, k2.

Rnd 21: P13, pfb, k2, p1, k1, ssk, p1, Right Leaf, k1, p2, k2.

Rnd 22: P15, k5, p2, k4, p2, k2.

Rnd 23: P15, ssk, k1, k2tog, p2, Inc-3, T4F, p1, k2.

Rnd 24: P15, k3, p2, k1, p1, k1, p2, k2, p1, k2.

Rnd 25: P15, S2KP2, p1, pfb, k1, M1R, p1, M1L, ssk, p1, T3F, k2.

Rnd 26: P19, k2, p1, k2, p2, k4.

Rnd 27: P18, pfb, k2, p1, k1, ssk, p1, T4F.

Rnd 28: P20, k5, p3, k2.

Rnd 29: P20, ssk, k1, k2tog, p1, p2tog, M1R, k2. 28 sts.

Rnd 30: P20, k3, p2, k3.

Rnd 31: P20, S2KP2, p2tog, k1, M1R, k2. 26 sts.

Rnd 32: P22, k4.

Rnd 33: P21, T3B, k2.

Rnd 34: P21, k2, p1, k2.

Rnd 35: P20, T3B, p1, k2.

Rnd 36: P19, T3B, p2, k2.

Rnd 37: P18, T3B, p3, k2.

Rnd 38: P24, k2.

Chart B

Rnd 1: {K2, p2} 5 times, k2, T4B.

Rnd 2: {K2, p2} 5 times, k4, p2.

Rnd 3: {K2, p2} 5 times, Left Leaf, p2.

Rnd 4: {K2, p2} 5 times, k3, p3.

Rnd 5: {K2, p2} 4 times, k2, T4B, Inc-3, p3. 28 sts.

Rnd 6: {K2, p2} 4 times, k4, p2, k1, p1, k1, p3.

Rnd 7: {K2, p2} 4 times, k1, T3B, p1, k2tog, M1R, p1, M1L, k1, pfb, p2. 30 sts.

Rnd 8: {K2, p2} 4 times, k3, p2, k2, p1, k2, p4.

Rnd 9: {K2, p2} 3 times, k2, p1, Left Leaf, p1, k2tog, k1, p1, k2, pfb, p3.

Rnd 10: {K2, p2} 3 times, k2, p1, k3, p2, k5, p5.

Rnd 11: {K2, p2} 3 times, k1, T4B, Inc-3, p2, ssk, k1, k2tog, p5.

Rnd 12: {K2, p2} 3 times, k3, p2, k1, p1, k1, p2, k3, p5.

Rnd 13: {K2, p2} 3 times, T3B, p1, k2tog, M1R, p1, M1L, k1, pfb, p1, S2KP2, p5.

Rnd 14: {K2, p2} 4 times, k2, p1, k2, p9.

Rnd 15: {K2, p2} twice, k2, Left Leaf, p1, k2tog, k1, p1, k2, pfb, p8.

Rnd 16: {K2, p2} twice, k5, p2, k5, p10.

Rnd 17: {K2, p2} twice, T4B, Inc-3, p2, ssk, k1, k2tog, p10.

Rnd 18: {K2, p2} 3 times, k1, p1, k1, p2, k3, p10.

Rnd 19: K2, p2, k2, p1, T3B, p1, k2tog, M1R, p1, M1L, k1, pfb, p1, S2KP2, p10.

Rnd 20: K2, {p2, k2, p1, k2} twice, p14.

Rnd 21: K2, p2, k1, Left Leaf, p1, k2tog, k1, p1, k2, pfb, p13.

Rnd 22: K2, p2, k4, p2, k5, p15.

Rnd 23: K2, p1, T4B, Inc-3, p2, ssk, k1, k2tog, p15.

Rnd 24: K2, p1, k2, p2, k1, p1, k1, p2, k3, p15.

Rnd 25: K2, T3B, p1, k2tog, M1R, p1, M1L, k1, pfb, p1, S2KP2, p15.

Rnd 26: K4, p2, k2, p1, k2, p19.

Rnd 27: T4B, p1, k2tog, k1, p1, k2, pfb, p18.

Rnd 28: K2, P3, k5, p20.

Rnd 29: K2, M1L, p2tog, p1, ssk, k1, k2tog, p20. 28 sts.

Rnd 30: K3, p2, k3, p20.

Rnd 31: K2, M1L, k1, p2tog, S2KP2, p20. 26 sts.

Rnd 32: K4, p22.

Rnd 33: K2, T3F, p21.

Rnd 34: K2, p1, k2, p21.

Rnd 35: K2, p1, T3F, p20.

Rnd 36: K2, p2, T3F, p19.

Rnd 37: K2, p3, T3F, p18.

Rnd 38: K2, p24.

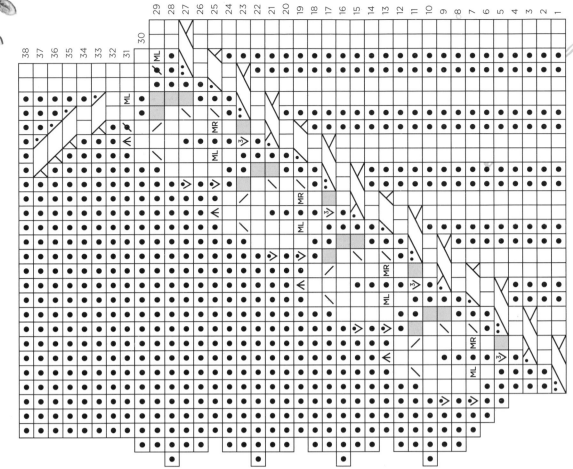

Chart B

Chart A

hanging leaves

A lovely lightweight shawl to wrap around your shoulders.
The plain Stockinette stitch body is adorned with an airy scalloped leaf border,
reminiscent of leaves clinging to branches at the end of the season.

{ FINISHED MEASUREMENTS }

Length: 65" / 165 cm from end to end
Width: 41" / 104 cm at widest point of center
including border

{ MATERIALS }

MC: 1 skein The Fibre Company *Meadow* [40% Merino,
25% Llama, 20% Silk, 15% Linen; 545 yd / 498 m
per 3½ oz / 100 g skein] in Lady Slipper OR approx 550 yd /
500 m of a lace or fingering weight wool

CC: 1 skein Shibui Knits *Cima* [70% Superbaby Alpaca,
30% Fine Merino Wool; 328 yd / 300 m
per 1¾ oz / 50 g skein] in Artichoke OR approx 125 yd /
100 m of a lace or fingering weight wool

Alternate Yarns: Malabrigo *Lace*, Madelinetosh *Tosh Lace*,
Madelinetosh *Prairie*

US5 / 3.75 mm 32" / 80 cm circular needle
US4 / 3.5 mm 32" / 80 cm circular needle

Stitch markers, tapestry needle

{ GAUGE }

20 sts and 32 rows over 4" / 10 cm in St st
on US5 / 3.75 mm needles
Or size needed for accurate gauge.

68

Body

With MC, CO 3 sts onto larger circular needle.

Knit 6 rows.

Pick up and knit 3 sts along vertical edge of rectangle in each of the 3 garter ridges. Pick up and knit 3 sts from CO edge. 9 sts.

Next row (WS): K3, p3, k3.
Inc row (RS): K4, M1R, M3, M1L, k4. 13 sts.
Next row (WS): K3, purl until 3 sts rem, k3.

Set up row (RS): K3, {pm, M1R, k1} 4 times, {M1L, pm, k1} 3 times, M1L, pm, k3. 8 markers placed. 21 sts.

Rows 1 and 3 (WS): K3, purl until 3 sts rem, slipping markers as you go, k3.
Row 2 (RS): Knit.
Row 4 (RS): {Knit to marker, sm, M1R} 4 times, {knit to marker, M1L, sm} 4 times, k3. 8 sts inc.

Rep last 4 rows 40 times more. 349 sts.

Switch to CC.

Purl 1 row, removing markers and inc 4 sts evenly. 353 sts.

Knit 1 row.

Border

NOTE: The following bind off results in one live stitch remaining on the needle followed by three bound-off stitches. This pattern is repeated across the row to the last stitch, which remains on the needle.

Set up row (WS): With smaller needles, p1, {p1,*p1, pass second st over first st loosely, rep from * twice more} 88 times. 89 sts.

NOTE: The border will now be worked using the first stitch, while the remaining 88 body stitches will be joined to the border at a rate of 2 stitches per leaf.

INDIVIDUAL LEAF

Row 1 (RS): K1, *{return st to left needle, k1-tbl} 6 times, return st to left needle, M3. 3 border sts.
Row 2 (WS): P1, k1, p1.
Row 3: K1, M1R, p1, M1L, k1. 5 sts.
Row 4: P2, k1, p2.
Row 5: {K1, M1R} twice, p1, {M1L, k1} twice. 9 sts.
Row 6: P4, k1, p4.

Row 7: K4, M1R, p1, M1L, k4. 11 sts.

Row 8: P5, k1, p5.

Row 9: K10, ssk border st with next body st.

Rows 10, 12, 14, 16, and 18 (WS): Purl.

Row 11: Ssk, k7, k2tog. 9 sts.

Row 13: Ssk, k5, k2tog. 7 sts.

Row 15: Ssk, k3, k2tog. 5 sts.

Row 17: Ssk, k1, k2tog. 3 sts.

Row 19: S2KP2, return last st to left needle, ssk border st with next body st. Return st to left needle. 1 border st.

Rep these 19 rows 43 times more. 44 leaves.

Finishing

Cut yarn. Weave in all ends on the WS. Wet block and pin leaves into place. Blocking is crucial to the shawl draping well and the leaves lying flat.

ivy trellis hat

Meandering cables and leaves climb up this beret like ivy on a trellis.
Complete your accessory wardrobe with the matching
Ivy Trellis Socks and *Ivy Trellis Mittens* from *Botanical Knits*.

{ SIZE }

Stretches to fit a 20–22" / 51–56 cm head circ

{ FINISHED MEASUREMENTS }

Brim circ: approx 18" / 46 cm, unstretched

{ MATERIALS }

1 skein Becoming Art *Theia MCS Sport* [75% Merino, 15% Cashmere, 10% Silk; 260 yd / 238 m per 4.02 oz / 114 g skein] in Morning Star OR approx 175 yd / 160 m of a sport weight wool or wool blend

Alternate Yarns: Madelinetosh *Tosh Sport*

US5 / 3.75 mm 16" / 40 cm circular needle
US6 / 4 mm 16" / 40 cm circular needle
and set of double-pointed needles

Stitch marker, cable needle, tapestry needle

{ GAUGE }

24 sts and 28 rows over 4" / 10 cm in St st worked in the rnd on US6 / 4 mm needles
Or size needed for accurate gauge.

Brim

CO 108 sts onto smaller circular needle. Pm, join for working in the rnd being careful not to twist your sts.

Ribbing set up rnd: {K2, p2, k1, p2, k2, p3, k3, p3}, rep.

Work in est rib patt for 1.5" / 4 cm.

Switch to larger circular needle.

Set up rnd: {K2, p2, k1, p2, k2, p1, pfb, p1, k3, p1, pfb, p1}, rep. 120 sts.

Work Rnds 1–16 of Chart A twice. Work Rnds 1–14 of Chart B once. Switch to dpns when work becomes too tight on the circular needle.

Finishing

Cut yarn, thread tail onto tapestry needle and pass through rem 12 sts and cinch to close. Weave in all ends on the WS. Wet block by stretching over a dinner plate.

Chart A (WORKED 6 TIMES AROUND)

Rnd 1: {K2, p2, Inc-3, p2, k2, p4, k3, p4}, rep. 132 sts.

Rnd 2: {K2, pfb, p1, k1, yo, p1, yo, k1, p1, pfb, k2, p4, S2KP2, p4}, rep. 144 sts.

Rnd 3: Remove marker, sl 2 sts from left needle to right needle, replace marker for new beg of rnd. {P3, k2, p1, k2, p3, C4F, p5, C4B}, rep.

Rnd 4: {Pfb, p2, k2, yo, p1, yo, k2, p2, pfb, k4, p5, k4}, rep. 168 sts.

Rnd 5: {P4, k3, p1, k3, p4, k2, T4F, p1, T4B, k2}, rep.

Rnd 6: {P4, ssk, k3, k2tog, p4, k2, p2, k2, p1, k2, p2, k2}, rep. 156 sts.

Rnd 7: {P4, k5, p4, k2, p2, Dec-5, p2, k2}, rep. 132 sts.

Rnd 8: {P4, ssk, k1, k2tog, p4, k2, p2, k1, p2, k2}, rep. 120 sts.

Rnd 9: {P4, k3, p4, k2, p2, Inc-3, p2, k2}, rep. 132 sts.

Rnd 10: {P4, S2KP2, p4, k2, pfb, p1, k1, yo, p1, yo, k1, p1, pfb, k2}, rep. On last rep, work until 2 sts rem on left needle. Sl 2 sts from left needle to right needle, remove marker, slip 2 sts back to left needle, replace marker for new beg of rnd. 144 sts.

Rnd 11: {C4F, p5, C4B, p3, k2, p1, k2, p3}, rep.

Rnd 12: {K4, p5, k4, pfb, p2, k2, yo, p1, yo, k2, p2, pfb}, rep. 168 sts.

Rnd 13: {K2, T4F, p1, T4B, k2, p4, k3, p1, k3, p4}, rep.

Rnd 14: {K2, p2, k2, p1, k2, p2, k2, p4, ssk, k3, k2tog, p4}, rep. 156 sts.

Rnd 15: {K2, p2, Dec-5, p2, k2, p4, k5, p4}, rep. 132 sts.

Rnd 16: {K2, p2, k1, p2, k2, p4, ssk, k1, k2tog, p4}, rep. 120 sts.

Chart B (WORKED 6 TIMES AROUND)

Rnd 1: {K2, p2, Inc-3, p2, k2, p4, k3, p4}, rep. 132 sts.

Rnd 2: {K2, p2, k1, yo, p1, yo, k1, p2, k2, p4, S2KP2, p4}, rep.

Rnd 3: Remove marker, sl 2 sts from left needle to right needle, replace marker for new beg of rnd. {P2, k2, p1, k2, p2, T4F, P5, T4B}, rep.

Rnd 4: {P2, k2, yo, p1, yo, k2, p4, k2, p5, k2, p2}, rep. 144 sts.

Rnd 5: {P2, k3, p1, k3, p4, T4F, p1, T4B, p2}, rep.

Rnd 6: {P2, ssk, k3, k2tog, p6, k2, k2tog, k1, p4}, rep. 126 sts.

Rnd 7: {P2, k5, p6, C4B, p6, k5, p6, C4F, p4}, rep 3 times.

Rnd 8: {P2, ssk, k1, k2tog, p5, T3B, T3F, p3}, rep 6 times. 114 sts.

Rnd 9: {P2, k3, p4, k2tog, k1, p2, k1, ssk, p2}, rep. 102 sts.

Rnd 10: {P2, S2KP2, p3, k2tog, k1, p2, k1, ssk, p1}, rep. 78 sts.

Rnd 11: {P5, k2tog, k1, p2tog, k1, ssk}, rep. 60 sts.

Rnd 12: Remove marker, sl 1 st from left needle to right needle, replace marker for new beg of rnd. {P3, k2tog, k1, p1, k1, ssk}, rep. 48 sts.

Rnd 13: Remove marker, sl 1 st from left needle to right needle, replace marker for new beg of rnd. {P1, k2tog, k1, p1, k1, ssk}, rep. 36 sts.

Rnd 14: Remove marker, sl 2 sts from left needle to right needle. {Dec-5, p1}, rep. 12 sts.

Chart A

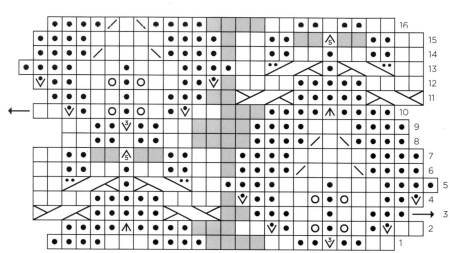

Chart B

☐	knit	⬚ T3B		T3B: Twist 3 Back
●	purl	⬚ T3F		T3F: Twist 3 Front
O	yo	⬚ C4B		C4B: Cable 4 Back
╱	k2tog	⬚ C4F		C4F: Cable 4 Front
╲	ssk	⬚ T4B		T4B: Twist 4 Back
⋀	S2KP2	⬚ T4F		T4F: Twist 4 Front

⬚ p2tog	←	Remove marker, sl 1 st from left needle to right needle, replace marker for new beg of rnd.
⬚ Dec-5	⟵	Sl 2 sts to the left as follows: Sl last 2 sts to next needle.
⬚ pfb	⟶	Sl 2 sts to the right as follows: Before working round, sl 2 sts from left needle to right needle; rep for each dpn.
⬚ Inc-3		
⬚ no stitch		

forest foliage

A semi-circular shawl featuring autumn leaves floating
amidst a sea of openwork lace stitches.
A delicate picot edging adds a feminine touch.

{ FINISHED MEASUREMENTS }

Length: approx 60" / 152.5 cm from end to end
Width: approx 26" / 66 cm at widest point of center
including border

{ MATERIALS }

2 skeins Madelinetosh *Tosh Merino Light*
[100% Superwash Merino Wool; 420 yd / 384 m
per 3½ oz / 100 g skein]; in Fig
OR approx 550 yd / 500 m of a lace weight
or fingering weight wool or wool blend

Alternate Yarn: Malabrigo *Sock*

US7 / 4.5 mm 32" / 80 cm circular needle

Stitch markers, tapestry needle

{ GAUGE }

20 sts and 28 rows over 4" / 10 cm in St st
on US7 / 4.5 mm needles
Or size needed for accurate gauge.

NOTES: Don't be fooled by the number and size of the charts for this pattern. They are really quite logical and easy to follow.

Chart A begins with three leaves—outlined in green—and establishes simple lace using yo-dec pairs between them. Chart B begins a new row of four leaves, while finishing the tips of the leaves worked in Chart A. The tips of the leaves from Chart A decrease into yo-S2KP2-yo sets that become the stems for the leaves worked in Chart C. The number of leaves increases with each chart until there are eight leaves in Chart F. The border begins in Chart G where a new motif is added in place of new leaves.

Each time a notch is formed on the sides of a leaf, a new yo-dec pair is added to the lace on either side. Because new leaves are added at the outer edge, the number of yo-dec pairs increases with each leaf or stem as you work across the row to the center repeated portion, and then decreases likewise as you work toward the left edge. You may find that after Chart C, you are able to read the lace pattern between the leaves and only use the green outlined portion of the charts for the leaves. If you choose to place markers on either side of the leaves, simply move both markers two stitches toward the center of the leaf each time a notch is formed.

Pattern

CO 11 sts.

Set up row (WS): K3, p5, k3.

Next row (RS): K3, k2tog, k1, ssk, k3. 9 sts.
Next row: K3, purl to last 3 sts, k3.

Work Chart A once, working rep section twice.

Work Chart B once, working rep section 3 times. Work Charts C through G once each consecutively as for Chart B. 329 sts.

Border

NOTE: The following bind-off results in single live stitches with one to three bound off stitches between them.

Row 115: K1, {k1, (k1, pass second st over first st loosely) twice} 2 times, *{k1, (k1, pass second st over first st loosely) 3 times} 7 times, (k2, pass second st over first st loosely) 4 times; rep from * 7 times more, {k1, (k1, pass second st over first st loosely) 3 times} 7 times, {k1, (k1, pass second st over first st loosely) twice) 2 times. 100 sts.

NOTE: The border is worked using a knitted chain stitch technique. Each time a stitch is slipped back to the left needle and worked, one chain stitch is formed. Each k2tog joins the current chain stitch with the next stitch from the previous row.

Row 116 (WS): K1, *{(slip last st back to left needle, k1) 8 times, slip last st back to left needle, k2tog} twice, {(slip last st back to left needle, k1) 10 times, slip last st back to left needle, k2tog} 3 times, (slip last st back to left needle, k1) 15 times, slip last st back to left needle, k2tog, {(slip last st back to left needle, k1) 10 times, slip last st back to left needle, k2tog} 3 times, {(slip last st back to left needle, k1) 8 times, slip last st back to left needle, k2tog} twice; rep from * 8 times more.

Finishing

Cut yarn. Weave in all ends on the WS. Wet block and pin to measurements. Place a pin to stretch each loop of the edging. Proper blocking is crucial to the shawl draping well and the leaves lying flat.

Legend

☐	knit RS rows, purl WS rows
●	purl RS rows, knit WS rows
⊠	k1-tbl
╲	k2tog
╱	ssk
◤	k3tog
◢	sssk
⬙	S2KP2
⬕	Dec-5
O	yo
ML	M1L
MR	M1R
⬙	M3
⬙	M5
▨	no stitch
☐	patt rep
⬚	leaf outline

Chart A

Chart B

Chart C

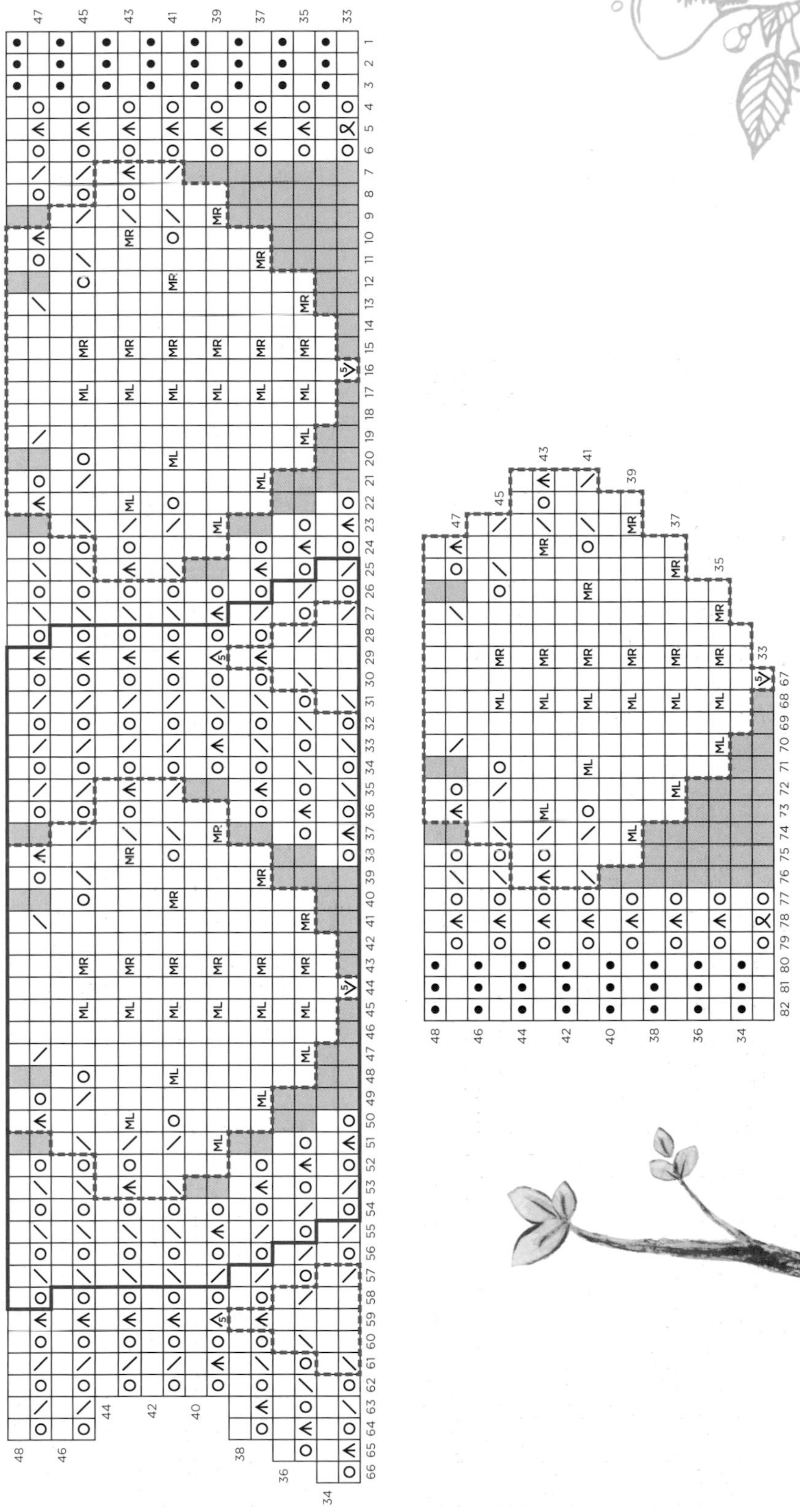

82

Chart D

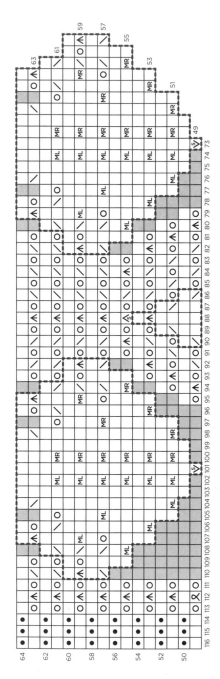

Chart E

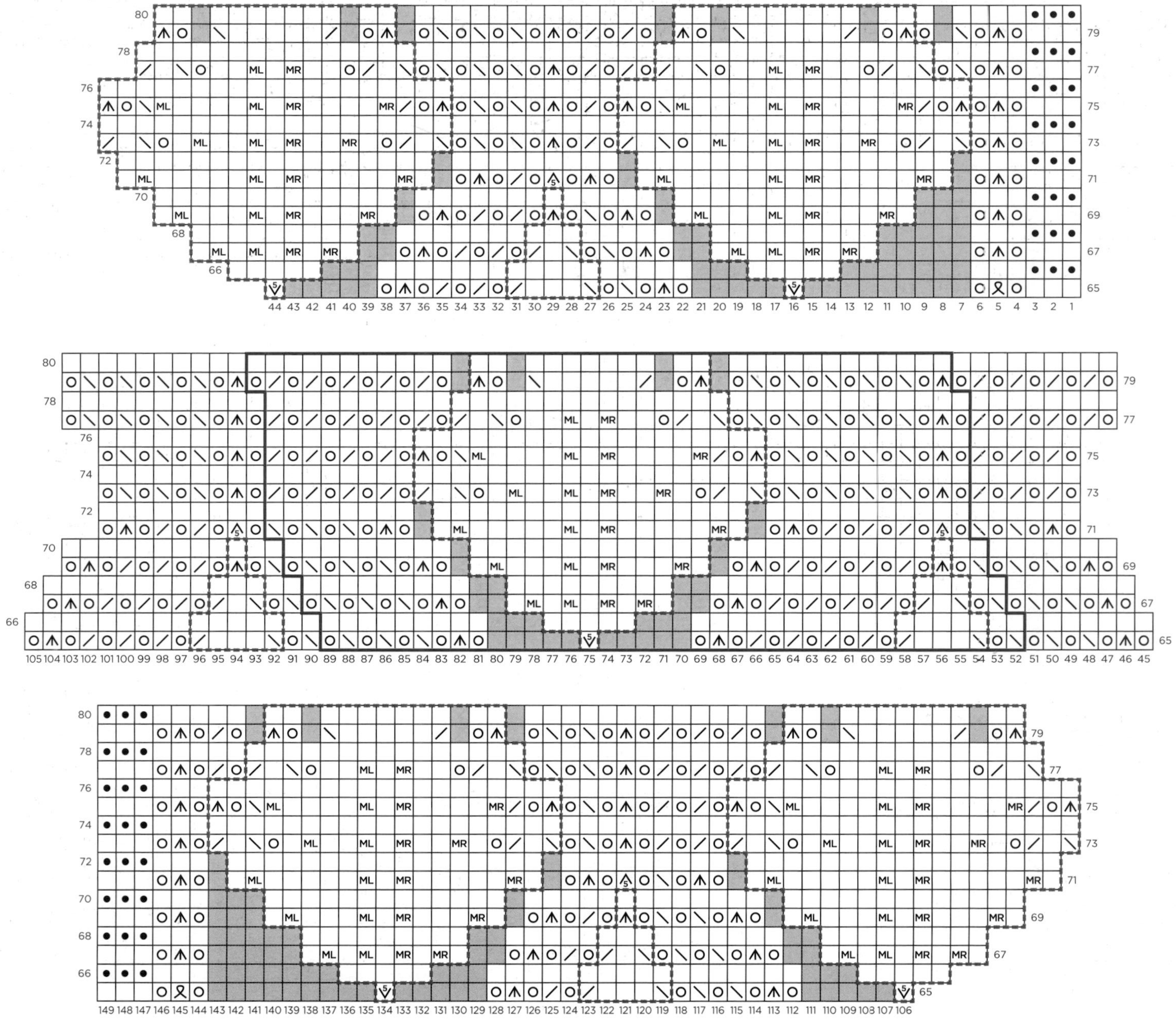

Chart F

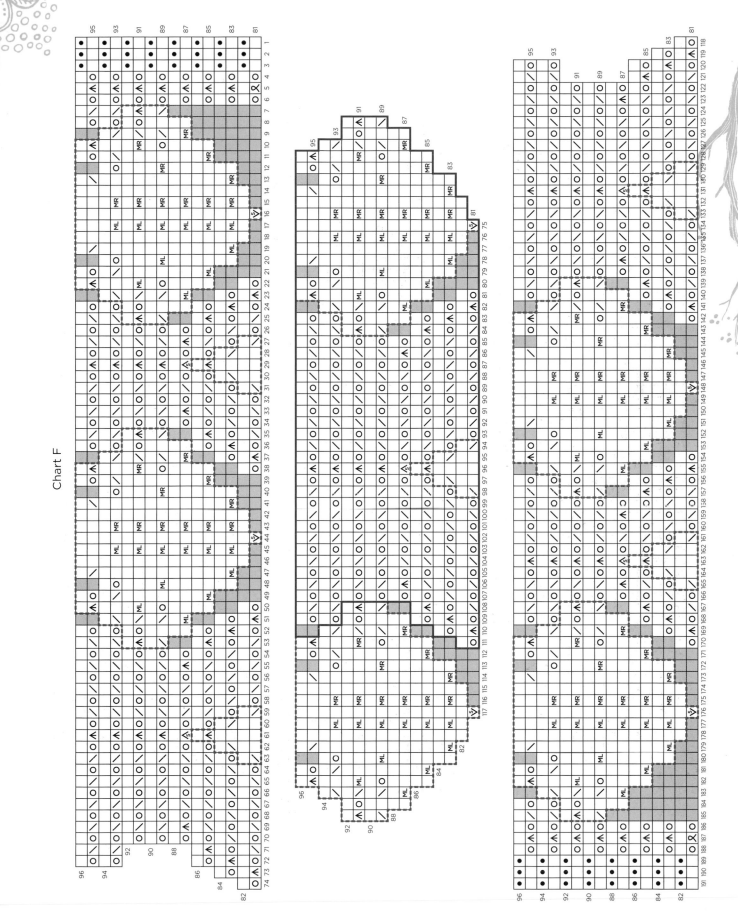

Chart G

Chart G, cont'd

life cycle

A long string of decorative leaves to wrap around your neck as a scarf and add color to your wardrobe. The gradient shades of the yarn correspond to the changing colors of leaves during their spring-to-autumn life cycle.

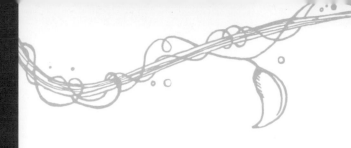

{ FINISHED MEASUREMENTS }

Length: 96" / 244 cm

Width: 4" / 10 cm

{ MATERIALS }

2 skeins Spincycle Yarns *Dyed in the Wool*

[100% Superwash Bluefaced Leicester Wool;

200 yd / 183 m per 2.6 oz / 75 g skein]

in End of Summer

OR approx 300 yd / 275 m

of a sport weight wool or wool blend

Alternate Yarn: Noro *Ayatori*

US7 / 4.5 mm straight needles

Tapestry needle

{ GAUGE }

20 sts and 28 rows over 4" / 10 cm in St st

on US7 / 4.5 mm needles

Or size needed for accurate gauge.

Pattern

CO 3 sts.

Set up row (WS): P3.

Work rows 1–42 of Chart once.

Rep rows 15–42 19 times more.

Work rows 43–52 once. 41 leaves.

Finishing

Cut yarn. Weave in all ends on the WS. Wet block.

Chart

Row 1 (RS): K1, M1R, p1, M1L, k1. 5 sts.

Row 2 (WS): P2, k1, p2.

Row 3: K1, M1R, k1, yo, p1, yo, k1, M1L, k1. 9 sts.

Row 4: P4, k1, p4.

Row 5: K1, M1R, k3, p1, k3, M1L, k1. 11 sts.

Row 6: P5, k1, p5.

Row 7: K1, M1R, k4, yo, p1, yo, k4, M1L, k1. 15 sts.

Row 8: P7, k1, p7.

Row 9: K1, M1R, k6, p1, k6, M1L, k1. 17 sts.

Row 10: P8, k1, p8.

Row 11: K8, yo, p1, yo, k8. 19 sts.

Row 12: P9, k1, p9.

Row 13: K9, M1R, p1, M1L, k9. 21 sts.

Row 14: P10, k1, p10.

Row 15: K1, M1R, p1, M1L, ssk, k5, sssk, k7, k2tog. 19 sts.

Row 16: P16, k1, p2.

Row 17: K1, M1R, k1, yo, p1, yo, k1, M1L, ssk, k3, sssk, k5, k2tog.

Row 18: P14, k1, p4.

Row 19: K1, M1R, k3, p1, k3, M1L, ssk, k1, sssk, k3, k2tog. 17 sts.

Row 20: P11, k1, p5.

Row 21: K1, M1R, k4, yo, p1, yo, k4, M1L, ssk, k3, k2tog. 19 sts.

Row 22: P11, k1, p7.

Row 23: K1, M1R, k6, p1, k6, M1L, ssk, k1, k2tog.

Row 24: P10, k1, p8.

Row 25: K8, yo, p1, yo, k7, ssk, k1. 20 sts.

Row 26: P10, k1, p9.

Row 27: K9, M1R, p1, M1L, k8, ssk. 21 sts.

Row 28: P10, k1, p10.

Row 29: Ssk, k7, k3tog, k5, k2tog, M1R, p1, M1L, k1. 19 sts.

Row 30: P2, k1, p16.

Row 31: Ssk, k5, k3tog, k3, k2tog, M1R, k1, yo, p1, yo, k1, M1L, k1.

Row 32: P4, k1, p14.

Row 33: Ssk, k3, k3tog, k1, k2tog, M1R, k3, p1, k3, M1L, k1. 17 sts.

Row 34: P5, k1, p11.

Row 35: Ssk, k3, k2tog, M1R, k4, yo, p1, yo, k4, M1L, k1. 19 sts.

Row 36: P7, k1, p11.

Row 37: Ssk, k1, k2tog, M1R, k6, p1, k6, M1L, k1.

Row 38: P8, k1, p10.

Row 39: K1, k2tog, k7, yo, p1, yo, k8. 20 sts.

Row 40: P9, k1, p10.

Row 41: K2tog, k8, M1R, p1, M1L, k9. 21 sts.

Row 42: P10, k1, p10.

Rep rows 15–42 19 times more.

Row 43: Ssk, k7, sssk, k7, k2tog. 17 sts.

Row 44: P17.

Row 45: Ssk, k5, sssk, k5, k2tog. 13 sts.

Row 46: P13.

Row 47: Ssk, k3, sssk, k3, k2tog. 9 sts.

Row 48: P3, p3tog-tbl, p3. 7 sts.

Row 49: Ssk, k3, k2tog. 5 sts.

Row 50: P5.

Row 51: Ssk, k1, k2tog. 3 sts.

Row 52: P3tog. 1 st.

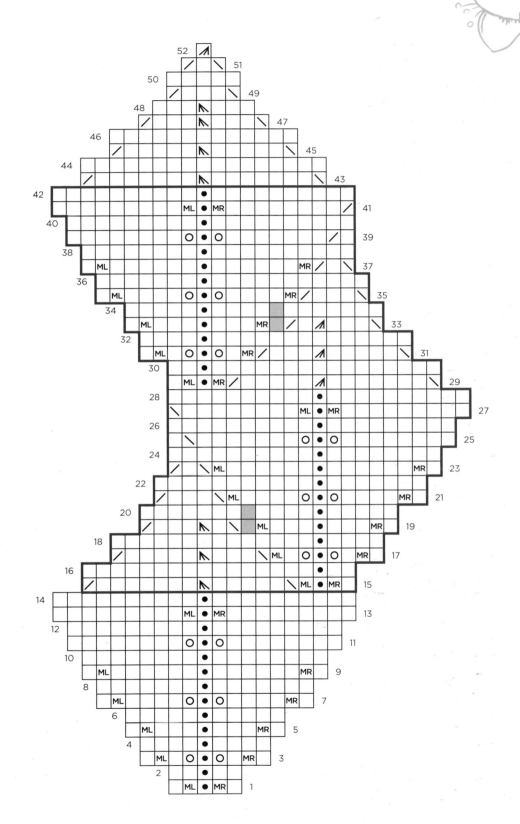

Chart

☐	knit RS rows, purl WS rows
⊡	purl RS rows, knit WS rows
Ⓞ	yo
ML	M1L
MR	M1R
╱	k2tog
╲	ssk
⫽	k3tog RS rows p3tog WS rows
⋀	sssk RS rows p3tog-tbl WS rows
▨	no stitch
☐	patt rep

thicket

A dense grouping of leaves form the stitch pattern of this lovely beret. *Thicket* begins at the brim and is knit upwards toward the crown.

{ SIZE }

Stretches to fit a 20–22" / 51–56 cm head circ

{ FINISHED MEASUREMENTS }

Brim circ: 18" / 46 cm unstretched

{ MATERIALS }

1 skein Juno Fibre Arts *Pearl*
[40% Superfine Alpaca, 40% Merino, 20% Silk;
251 yd / 230 m per 3½ oz / 100 g skein] in Touch Wood
OR approx 150 yd / 140 m of a dk weight wool
or wool blend

Alternate Yarn: Madelinetosh *Tosh Merino DK*

US4 / 3.5 mm 16" / 40 cm circular needle
US6 / 4 mm 16" / 40 cm circular needle
and set of double-pointed needles

Stitch marker, tapestry needle

{ GAUGE }

22 sts and 28 rows over 4" / 10 cm in St st
worked in the rnd on US6 / 4 mm needles
Or size needed for accurate gauge.

Brim

CO 120 sts onto smaller circular needle. Pm, join for working in the rnd being careful not to twist your sts.

Ribbing set up rnd: {K1, p1}, rep.

Work even in est rib patt for 1.5"/ 4 cm.

Switch to larger circular needle.

Knit 1 rnd.

Work Rnds 1–12 of Chart A twice then Rnds 1-6 once more. Work Rnds 1–15 of Chart B once. Switch to dpns when work becomes too tight on the circular needle.

Next rnd: K2tog, k8. 9 sts.
Next rnd: {S2KP2} 3 times. 3 sts. Remove marker.

Work 2 rnds of I-cord.

Finishing

Cut yarn, thread tail onto tapestry needle, pass through remaining 3 live sts and cinch to close.

Weave in all ends on the WS. Wet block, stretching over a dinner plate to dry.

Chart A (WORKED 5 TIMES AROUND)

Rnd 1: {K1, yo, ssk, k4, k2tog, k3, M1R, k1, M1L, k3, ssk, k4, k2tog, yo}, rep.

All even rnds 2–12: Knit unless otherwise specified.

Rnd 3: {K1, yo, k1, ssk, k2, k2tog, k4, M1R, k1, M1L, k4, ssk, k2, k2tog, k1, yo}, rep.

Rnd 5: {K1, yo, k2, ssk, k2tog, k5, M1R, k1, M1L, k5, ssk, k2tog, k2, yo}, rep.

Rnd 7: {K1, M1L, k3, ssk, k4, k2tog, yo, k1, yo, ssk, k4, k2tog, k3, M1R}, rep.

Rnd 9: {K1, M1L, k4, ssk, k2, k2tog, k1, yo, k1, yo, k1, ssk, k2, k2tog, k4, M1R}, rep.

Rnd 11: {K1, M1L, k5, ssk, k2tog, k2, yo, k1, yo, k2, ssk, k2tog, k5, M1R}, rep.

Chart B (WORKED 5 TIMES AROUND)

Rnd 1: {K1, M1L, k3, ssk, k5, S2KP2, k5, k2tog, k3, M1R}, rep. 110 sts.

All even rnds 2–14: Knit unless otherwise specified.

Rnd 3: {K1, M1L, k4, ssk, k3, S2KP2, k3, k2tog, k4, M1R}, rep. 100 sts.

Rnd 5: {K1, M1L, k5, ssk, k1, S2KP2, k1, k2tog, k5, M1R}, rep. 90 sts.

Rnd 7: {K8, S2KP2, k7}, rep. 80 sts.

Rnd 8: Move marker 4 sts to the left as follows: Remove marker, k4, pm for new beg of rnd, knit to end of rnd.

Rnd 9: {K3, S2KP2, k2}, rep. 60 sts.

Rnd 10: Knit.

Rnd 11: {K2, S2KP2, k1}, rep. 40 sts.

Rnd 12: Knit.

Rnd 13: {K1, S2KP2}, rep. 20 sts.

Rnd 14: Knit.

Rnd 15: {S2KP2, k1} twice, rep. 10 sts.

Chart A

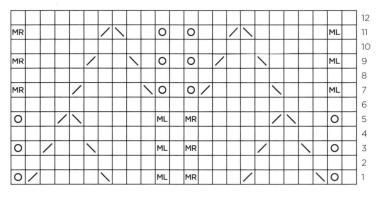

Chart B

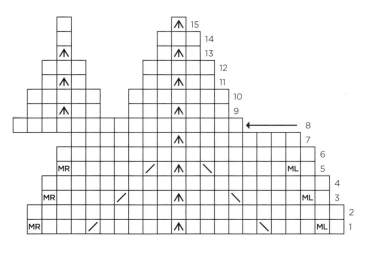

☐	knit RS rows, purl WS rows	∕	k2tog	ML M1L
⊡	purl RS rows, knit WS rows	∖	ssk	MR M1R
○	yo	⋀	S2KP2	← Remove marker, k4, place marker for new beg of rnd.

verdure

Simple, cozy fingerless mitts with a sprouting plant motif
decorating the top of the hand.

{ SIZE }
Women's Medium

{ FINISHED MEASUREMENTS }
Width: approx 7½" / 19 cm around at widest point of hand
Length: 8½" / 21.5 cm

{ MATERIALS }
1 skein Madelinetosh *Tosh DK* [100% Merino;
225 yd / 206 m per oz / 100 g skein] in Grove
OR approx 150 yd / 140 m of a dk weight wool
or wool blend

Alternate Yarn: Madelinetosh *Tosh Merino DK*,
Cascade Yarns *220*

Set of US6 / 4 mm double-pointed needles

Stitch markers in 2 different colors,
cable needle, stitch holder, tapestry needle

{ GAUGE }
20 sts and 30 rows over 4" / 10 cm in St st
worked in the rnd on US6 / 4 mm needles
Or size needed for accurate gauge.

Cuff

CO 37 sts onto 1 dpn. Divide sts evenly among 3 dpns. Pm, join for working in the rnd being careful not to twist your sts.

Ribbing set up rnd: {K1-tbl, p1} 9 times, k2-tbl, p1, {k1-tbl, p1} 8 times.

Work even in est rib patt for 1½" / 4 cm.

Hand

LEFT MITT ONLY
Rnd 1: K9, pm (contrasting color), work Rnd 1 of Chart A over 20 sts, pm (contrasting color), knit to end.
Rnds 2–20: Knit to marker, work chart as est to marker, knit to end.
Rnd 21: K8, M1R, k1, M1L, sm, work Rnd 21 of Chart A, knit to end.
Rnds 22, 24, 26, 28 and 30: Knit to marker, work chart as est to marker, knit to end.
Rnd 23: K8, M1R, k3, M1L, sm, work Rnd 23 of Chart A, knit to end.
Rnd 25: K8, M1R, k5, M1L, sm, work Rnd 25 of Chart A, knit to end.
Rnd 27: K8, M1R, k7, M1L, sm, work Rnd 27 of Chart A, knit to end.
Rnd 29: K8, M1R, k9, M1L, sm, work Rnd 29 of Chart A, knit to end.
Rnd 31: K8, M1R, k11, M1L, sm, work Rnd 31 of Chart A, knit to end.
Rnd 32: K8, slide next 13 sts onto st holder to be worked later, CO 1 st, sm, work Chart A as est to marker, knit to end.
Rnds 33–41: Knit to marker, work Chart A as est to marker, knit to end.

RIGHT MITT ONLY
Rnd 1: K9, pm, work Rnd 1 of Chart B over 20 sts, pm, knit to end.
Rnds 2–20: Knit to marker, work chart as est to marker, knit to end.
Rnd 21: Knit to marker, work Rnd 21 of Chart B, sm, M1R, k1, M1L, knit to end.
Rnds 22, 24, 26, 28 and 30: Knit to marker, work chart as est to marker, knit to end.
Rnd 23: Knit to marker, work Rnd 23 of Chart B, sm, M1R, k3, M1L, knit to end.
Rnd 25: Knit to marker, work Rnd 25 of Chart B, sm, M1R, k5, M1L, knit to end.
Rnd 27: Knit to marker, work Rnd 27 of Chart B, sm, M1R, k7, M1L, knit to end.
Rnd 29: Knit to marker, work Rnd 29 of Chart B, sm, M1R, k9, M1L, knit to end.
Rnd 31: Knit to marker, work Rnd 31 of Chart B, sm, M1R, k11, M1L, knit to end.
Rnd 32: Knit to marker, work Chart B as est to marker, slide next 13 sts onto st holder to be worked later, CO 1 st, knit to end.
Rnds 33–41: Knit to marker, work Chart B as est to marker, knit to end.

BOTH MITTS

Remove contrasting color markers. Cont in est patt for 5 rnds more.

Ribbing set up rnd: {P1, k1-tbl}, rep.

Cont in est rib patt for 3 rnds more.

BO in rib. Remove marker. Cut yarn.

Thumb

Return 13 held sts to dpns and divide evenly among 3 needles. Rejoin yarn.

Rnd 1: K13, pick up and knit 1 st on left side of thumb opening, 1 middle st in previous CO, and 1 more st on right side of thumb opening. Pm to mark the beg of rnd. 16 sts.
Rnd 2: K13, k3-tbl.

Knit 2 rnds.

Ribbing set up rnd: {K1-tbl, p1}, rep.

Cont in est rib patt for 3 rnds more.

BO in rib. Remove marker.

Finishing

Cut yarn. Weave in all ends on the WS. Wet block.

Chart A

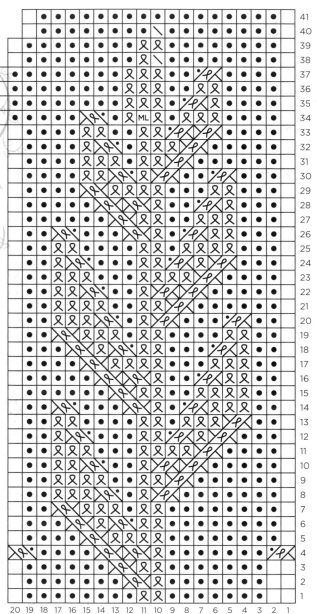

Chart B

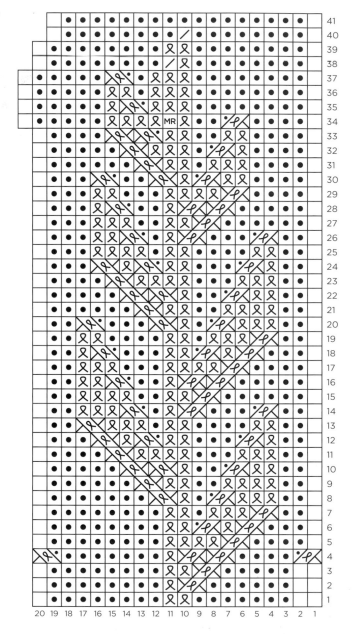

☐	knit	

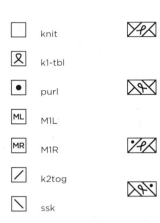

☒ k1-tbl

● purl

ML M1L

MR M1R

╱ k2tog

╲ ssk

C2B-tbl: Cable 2 Back through the back loop. Sl 1 st to cn and hold to back. K1-tbl from left needle, then k1 from cn.

C2F-tbl: Cable 2 Front through the back loop. Sl 1 st to cn and hold to front. K1 from left needle, then k1-tbl from cn.

T2B-tbl: Twist 2 Back through the back loop. Sl 1 st to cn and hold to back. K1-tbl from left needle, then p1 from cn.

T2F-tbl: Twist 2 Front through the back loop. Sl 1 st to cn and hold to front. P1 from left needle, then k1-tbl from cn.

106 Chart A

Rnd 1: K2, p7, k2-tbl, p7, k2.

Rnd 2: K2, p7, k1-tbl, C2F-tbl, p6, k2.

Rnd 3: K2, p7, k2-tbl, C2F-tbl, p5, k2.

Rnd 4: T2B, p7, k1-tbl, {C2F-tbl} twice, p4, T2F.

Rnd 5: K1, p8, k4-tbl, C2F-tbl, p4, k1.

Rnd 6: K1, p8, k2-tbl, T2F-tbl, k1-tbl, C2F-tbl, p3, k1.

Rnd 7: K1, p8, k2-tbl, p1, k3-tbl, C2F-tbl, p2, k1.

Rnd 8: K1, p7, C2B-tbl, k1-tbl, p1, T2F-tbl, k3-tbl, p2, k1.

Rnd 9: K1, p6, C2B-tbl, k2-tbl, p2, k4-tbl, p2, k1.

Rnd 10: K1, p5, C2B-tbl twice, k1-tbl, p2, T2F-tbl, k2-tbl, p2, k1.

Rnd 11: K1, p4, C2B-tbl, k4-tbl, p3, k3-tbl, p2, k1.

Rnd 12: K1, p3, C2B-tbl, k1-tbl, T2B-tbl, k2-tbl, p3, T2F-tbl, k1-tbl, p2, k1.

Rnd 13: K1, p2, C2B-tbl, k3-tbl, p1, k2-tbl, p4, k2-tbl, p2, k1.

Rnd 14: K1, p2, k3-tbl, T2B-tbl, p1, k1-tbl, C2F-tbl, p3, T2F-tbl, p2, k1.

Rnd 15: K1, p2, k4-tbl, p2, k2-tbl, C2F-tbl, p6, k1.

Rnd 16: K1, p2, k2-tbl, T2B-tbl, p2, k1-tbl, {C2F-tbl} twice, p5, k1.

Rnd 17: K1, p2, k3-tbl, p3, k4-tbl, C2F-tbl, p4, k1.

Rnd 18: K1, p2, k1-tbl, T2B-tbl, p3, k2-tbl, T2F-tbl, k1-tbl, C2F-tbl, p3, k1.

Rnd 19: K1, p2, k2-tbl, p4, k2-tbl, p1, k3-tbl, C2F-tbl, p2, k1.

Rnd 20: K1, p2, T2B-tbl, p3, C2B-tbl, k1-tbl, p1, T2F-tbl, k3-tbl, p2, k1.

Rnd 21: K1, p6, C2B-tbl, k2-tbl, p2, k4-tbl, p2, k1.

Rnd 22: K1, p5, C2B-tbl twice, k1-tbl, p2, T2F-tbl, k2-tbl, p2, k1.

Rnd 23: K1, p4, C2B-tbl, k4-tbl, p3, k3-tbl, p2, k1.

Rnd 24: K1, p3, C2B-tbl, k1-tbl, T2B-tbl, k2-tbl, p3, T2F-tbl, k1-tbl, p2, k1.

Rnd 25: K1, p3, k4-tbl, p1, k2-tbl, p4, k2-tbl, p2, k1.

Rnd 26: K1, p3, k2-tbl, T2B-tbl, p1, k1-tbl, C2F-tbl, p3, T2F-tbl, p2, k1.

Rnd 27: K1, p3, k3-tbl, p2, k2-tbl, C2F-tbl, p6, k1.

Rnd 28: K1, p3, k1-tbl, T2B-tbl, p2, k1-tbl, C2F-tbl twice, p5, k1.

Rnd 29: K1, p3, k2-tbl, p3, k4-tbl, C2F-tbl, p4, k1.

Rnd 30: K1, p3, T2B-tbl, p2, C2B-tbl, k1-tbl, T2F-tbl, k2-tbl, p4, k1.

Rnd 31: K1, p6, C2B-tbl, k2-tbl, p1, k3-tbl, p4, k1.

Rnd 32: K1, p5, C2B-tbl, k3-tbl, p1, T2F-tbl, k1-tbl, p4, k1.

Rnd 33: K1, p4, C2B-tbl, T2B-tbl, k2-tbl, p2, k2-tbl, p4, k1.

Rnd 34: K1, p4, k3-tbl, p1, k1-tbl, M1L, k1-tbl, p2, T2F-tbl, p4, k1. 21 sts.

Rnd 35: K1, p4, k1-tbl, T2B-tbl, p1, k3-tbl, p8, k1.

Rnd 36: K1, p4, k2-tbl, p2, k3-tbl, p8, k1.

Rnd 37: K1, p4, T2B-tbl, p2, k3-tbl, p8, k1.

Rnd 38: K1, p8, ssk, k1-tbl, p8, k1. 20 sts.

Rnd 39: K1, p8, k2-tbl, p8, k1.

Rnd 40: K1, p8, ssk, p8, k1. 19 sts.

Rnd 41: K1, p17, k1.

Chart B

Rnd 1: K2, p7, k2-tbl, p7, k2.

Rnd 2: K2, p6, C2B-tbl, k1-tbl p7, k2.

Rnd 3: K2, p5, C2B-tbl, k2-tbl, p7, k2.

Rnd 4: T2B, p4,C2B-tbl twice, k1-tbl, p7, T2F.

Rnd 5: K1, p4, C2B-tbl, k4-tbl, p8, k1.

Rnd 6: K1, p3, C2B-tbl, k1-tbl, T2B-tbl, k2-tbl, p8, k1.

Rnd 7: K1, p2, C2B-tbl, k3-tbl, p1, k2-tbl, p8, k1.

Rnd 8: K1, p2, k3-tbl, T2B-tbl, p1, k1-tbl, C2F-tbl, p7, k1.

Rnd 9: K1, p2, k4-tbl, p2, k2-tbl, C2F-tbl, p6, k1.

Rnd 10: K1, p2, k2-tbl, T2B-tbl, p2, k1-tbl, C2F-tbl twice, p5, k1.

Rnd 11: K1, p2, k3-tbl, p3, k4-tbl, C2F-tbl, p4, k1.

Rnd 12: K1, p2, k1-tbl, T2B-tbl, p3, k2-tbl, T2F-tbl, k1-tbl, C2F-tbl, p3, k1.

Rnd 13: K1, p2, k2-tbl, p4, k2-tbl, p1, k3-tbl, C2F-tbl, p2, k1.

Rnd 14: K1, p2, T2B-tbl, p3, C2B-tbl, k1-tbl, p1, T2F-tbl, k3-tbl, p2, k1.

Rnd 15: K1, p6, C2B-tbl, k2-tbl, p2, k4-tbl, p2, k1.

Rnd 16: K1, p5, C2B-tbl twice, k1-tbl, p2, T2F-tbl, k2-tbl, p2, k1.

Rnd 17: K1, p4, C2B-tbl, k4-tbl, p3, k3-tbl, p2, k1.

Rnd 18: K1, p3, C2B-tbl, k1-tbl, T2B-tbl, k2-tbl, p3, T2F-tbl, k1-tbl, p2, k1.

Rnd 19: K1, p2, C2B-tbl, k3-tbl, p1, k2-tbl, p4, k2-tbl, p2, k1.

Rnd 20: K1, p2, k3-tbl, T2B-tbl, p1, k1-tbl, C2F-tbl, p3, T2F-tbl, p2, k1.

Rnd 21: K1, p2, k4-tbl, p2, k2-tbl, C2F-tbl, p6, k1.

Rnd 22: K1, p2, k2-tbl, T2B-tbl, p2, k1-tbl, C2F-tbl twice, p5, k1.

Rnd 23: K1, p2, k3-tbl, p3, k4-tbl, C2F-tbl, p4, k1.

Rnd 24: K1, p2, k1-tbl, T2B-tbl, p3, k2-tbl, T2F-tbl, k1-tbl, C2F-tbl, p3, k1.

Rnd 25: K1, p2, k2-tbl, p4, k2-tbl, p1, k4-tbl, p3, k1.

Rnd 26: K1, p2, T2B-tbl, p3, C2B-tbl, k1-tbl, p1, T2F-tbl, k2-tbl, p3, k1.

Rnd 27: K1, p6, C2B-tbl, k2-tbl, p2, k3-tbl, p3, k1.

Rnd 28: K1, p5, C2B-tbl twice, k1-tbl, p2, T2F-tbl, k1-tbl, p3, k1.

Rnd 29: K1, p4, C2B-tbl, k4-tbl, p3, k2-tbl, p3, k1.

Rnd 30: K1, p4, k2-tbl, T2B-tbl, k1-tbl, C2F-tbl, p2, T2F-tbl, p3, k1.

Rnd 31: K1, p4, k3-tbl, p1, k2-tbl, C2F-tbl, p6, k1.

Rnd 32: K1, p4, k1-tbl, T2B-tbl, p1, k3-tbl, C2F-tbl, p5, k1.

Rnd 33: K1, p4, k2-tbl, p2, k2-tbl, T2F-tbl, C2F-tbl, p4, k1.

Rnd 34: K1, p4, T2B-tbl, p2, k1-tbl, M1R, k1-tbl, p1, k3-tbl, p4, k1. 21 sts.

Rnd 35: K1, p8, k3-tbl, p1, T2F-tbl, k1-tbl, p4, k1.

Rnd 36: K1, p8, k3-tbl, p2, k2-tbl, p4, k1.

Rnd 37: K1, p8, k3-tbl, p2, T2F-tbl, p4, k1.

Rnd 38: K1, p8, k1-tbl, k2tog, p8, k1. 20 sts.

Rnd 39: K1, p8, k2-tbl, p8, k1.

Rnd 40: K1, p8, k2tog, p8, k1. 19 sts.

Rnd 41: K1, p17, k1.

TECHNIQUES

BACKWARDS LOOP CAST ON: Hold the needle in right hand. With left hand, wrap the strand of yarn connected to the ball around thumb counterclockwise, and hold the strand of yarn loosely in place against the palm of hand with remaining fingers.

*Slip the tip of your needle under the strand of yarn wrapped on the outermost edge of thumb. The needle will now have an extra loop on it. 1 stitch has been cast on. Tighten up the loop and repeat from * until the needle has the required amount of stitches.

I-CORD: *Knit to end, slide stitches to opposite end of double-pointed needle (do not turn); repeat from *.

KITCHENER STITCH: An invisible technique also known as "grafting" for seaming up live stitches on horizontal rows. Although traditionally used to seam up the toe of a sock, this technique is used to seam up the hood in the *Bare Branches* coat. Thread tail of yarn onto tapestry needle. Place the two double-pointed needles with the remaining stitches next to one another, with the wrong sides of the fabric facing in.

Set up: Slide the tapestry needle into the first stitch on the front needle as if to purl. Leave the stitch on the needle and pull the yarn snug. Slide the tapestry needle through the first stitch on the back needle as if to knit. Leave the stitch on the needle and pull the yarn snug.

Step 1: Slide the tapestry needle into the first stitch on the front needle again as if to knit. Pull the yarn snug and this time, slide the stitch off of the needle. Slide the tapestry needle into the next stitch on the front needle as if to purl. Leave the stitch on the needle and pull the yarn snug.

Step 2: Slide the tapestry needle into the first stitch on the back needle again as if to purl. Pull the yarn snug and this time, slide the stitch off of the needle. Slide the tapestry needle into the next stitch on the back needle as if to knit. Leave the stitch on the needle and pull the yarn snug. Repeat steps 1 and 2 for all stitches.

PICK UP AND KNIT: Slide needle under both strands of the stitch on the designated edge. Wrap yarn around the needle clockwise and pull a loop through. Repeat across the edge for the required amount of stitches.

REVERSE STOCKINETTE STITCH: Purl on the right side, knit on the wrong side when working flat. Purl all stitches when working in the round.

SHORT ROWS: Also known as wrap and turn (w&t).

Right side or knit stitch: Work in pattern to the stitch to be wrapped, move yarn to front of work and slip next stitch as if to knit. Bring yarn to back and turn work to other side. With wrong side facing, slip same stitch back to right needle as if to purl. Proceed to work across row in pattern.

Wrong side or purl stitch: Work in pattern to the stitch to be wrapped, move yarn to back of work and slip next stitch as if to purl. Bring yarn to front and turn work to other side. With right side facing, slip same stitch back to right needle as if to purl. Proceed to work across row in pattern.

The resulting wrap will look like a "necklace" or "noose" around your stitch.

Picking up wraps: Pull each wrap over to the wrong side of your work as follows:

Right side or knit stitch: Work to previously wrapped stitch. Insert right needle tip under wrap from the bottom up. Pull it up and over the stitch it was wrapping and onto the needle. The wrap will now be behind the stitch on the left needle. Knit both the stitch and the wrap together through the back loop. The wrap should be completely invisible from the right side.

Wrong side or purl stitch: Work to previously wrapped stitch. Insert right needle tip under wrap on the right side of your work from the bottom up (just as for the right side instructions). Since the wrong side is facing you, you will have to twist your work to do this. Pull it up and over the stitch it was wrapping towards the wrong side that is facing you and onto the needle. The wrap will now be behind the stitch on the left needle. Purl both the stitch and the wrap together. The wrap should be completely invisible from the right side.

STOCKINETTE STITCH: Knit on the right side, purl on the wrong side when working flat. Knit all stitches when working in the round.

THREE-NEEDLE BIND OFF: See Seaming.

WORK EVEN (AS ESTABLISHED): Work stitches in pattern as they appear without increasing or decreasing.

FINISHING

Proper finishing techniques give a crisp, professional look to your finished garment. Messy seams or unblocked pieces will not properly accentuate all of your hard work. You will not want to rush through or skip these final steps.

SEAMING: For a sweater worked in pieces, I recommend the following techniques for sewing your sweater pieces together: the three-needle bind off method for seaming up the shoulders, the vertical mattress stitch for side and sleeve seams, and the horizontal to vertical mattress stitch to set in the sweater sleeve to the armhole opening. When seaming, always try to use the tails left over from the cast on or bind off edges. Using up these tails will save you the hassle of having to weave them in later.

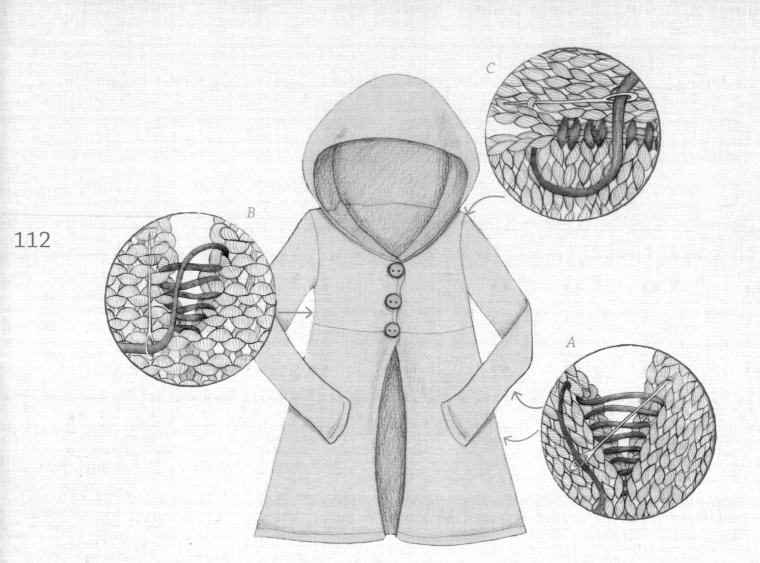

THREE-NEEDLE BIND OFF: A sturdy seam that conveniently does not require the use of a tapestry needle. You will use this technique when connecting the shoulders of the *Bare Branches* coat, *Flourish* cardigan and *Sunlit Autumn* cardigan.

Begin by placing the two double-pointed needles with the remaining stitches next to one another with the wrong sides of the fabric facing in. *Slide a third double-pointed needle through the first stitch on the front needle and the first stitch on the back needle as if to knit. Wrap yarn around the needle clockwise and knit through both of these stitches. There is now one stitch on the third double-pointed needle. Repeat from * once more. When there are two stitches on the third double-pointed needle, lift the first stitch over the second stitch and off of the needle, as you would in a normal bind off. Repeat across remaining stitches.

MATTRESS STITCH: An invisible technique that is perfect for the side and sleeve seams of a sweater. Begin with creating a neat join at the bottom edge of a seam. Insert your threaded tapestry needle first into the bottom corner stitch of one side from back to front, then to the opposite side in the same manner from back to front and tighten. This creates a figure eight in the process and blends in with the existing edge.

112

Seam Two Vertical Stockinette Stitch Pieces (A): You will use this technique when seaming up the sleeves and sides of the *Bare Branches* coat, *Flourish* cardigan and *Sunlit Autumn* cardigan. Begin by locating the last vertical row of knitting on the very edge of your work. By pulling gently and stretching this row, you will find little horizontal bars of yarn resembling a ladder connecting this row to the rest of the fabric. Stitch underneath these bars to connect the two pieces of fabric together. Slide your threaded tapestry needle under the first bar from the bottom up. Now find the corresponding bar on the second piece of fabric and repeat. Go back and forth between fabric pieces working in the corresponding bars, but keep the yarn loose. Pull the yarn to tighten after working ten bars or so, and watch the fabric come together invisibly as the seam disappears before your very eyes!

Seam Two Vertical Reverse Stockinette Stitch Pieces (B): This technique is used at the bodice portion of the *Bare Branches* coat along with the pocket seaming on the wrong side of the *Sunlit Autumn* cardigan. With Reverse Stockinette stitch fabric, you will see the stitches are made of a series of top and bottom loops or bumps snugly sitting beside each other. To seam up the reverse side, you will use the same basic technique outlined above, but instead slip your threaded tapestry needle underneath these loops making up the stitches. You will stitch underneath the top loops on one side and corresponding bottom loops on the other side. Continue seaming up the vertical line of either the respective top or bottom loops in the same manner.

Seam Horizontal Bound-Off Edges to Vertical Rows (C): You will use this technique when setting in the sleeves of the *Bare Branches* coat, *Flourish* cardigan and *Sunlit*

Autumn cardigan. Begin by lining up the shoulder seam to the center of the bound-off edge of the sweater sleeve cap. With your threaded tapestry needle, alternate between stitching into the vertical bars of the armhole opening and slipping the needle under both legs of the stitch below the bound-off edge of the sweater sleeve cap. You may have to pick up two vertical bars occasionally to make the stitches line up appropriately.

WEAVING IN ENDS: If there are any additional ends to weave in, thread them onto a tapestry needle and weave in a zig-zag fashion along the seam lines or edge on the wrong side of your work. If you carefully split the yarn strand of the stitch you are weaving into, this will help to stabilize the woven-in end and keep it from unraveling in the future.

BLOCKING: There are several methods used to block your finished knits. I prefer the wet blocking method, where I give each item a good soak before squeezing out excess water and pinning it out to dry flat. Blocking in this way smooths out any uneven stitches and really allows you to manipulate the knitted fabric into the shape you want. When blocking a hand-knit item, be sure to block to the measurements listed in the accompanying pattern schematic for your size. A lace shawl, however, should be stretched severely before pinning, to open up the lace stitches and really show off the pattern.

Commercial blocking boards and blocking wires are useful tools, but not absolutely necessary. You can successfully block your item using towels, a tape measure and t-pins. You will be amazed by what blocking can accomplish and how it can transform a knitted item. Stitches will be evened out and stitch patterns enhanced. Your hand-knit item will be clean, crisp and perfectly formed.

ABBREVIATIONS

approx: approximately

beg: begin(s)(ning)

BO: Bind Off

C4B: Cable 4 Back. Slip 2 sts to cable needle and hold to back. K2 from left needle, then k2 from cable needle.

C4F: Cable 4 Front. Slip 2 sts to cable needle and hold to front. K2 from left needle, then k2 from cable needle.

CO: Cast On

circ: circumference

cont: continue

cm: centimeter(s)

cn: cable needle

dec: decreas(ed)(es)(ing)

Dec-5: Decrease 5. Slip 3 sts with yarn in back. *Pass 2nd st on right needle over the 1st (center st). Slip the center st back to left needle and pass the 2nd st on left needle over it. Slip the center st back to right needle again and rep from * once more. Pick up yarn and knit center st tbl.

dpn(s): double-pointed needle(s)

est: established

inc: increas(ed)(es)(ing)

Inc-3: Increase 3. Knit through the back loop and then through the front loop of the same st. Insert left needle point behind the vertical strand that runs downward between the 2 sts just made and k1-tbl into this strand to make the 3rd st.

k: knit

k1-tbl: knit through the back loop

k2tog: Insert needle through next 2 sts as if to knit. Knit together.

k3tog: Insert needle through next 3 sts as if to knit. Knit together.

kfb: knit into front and back of st

M3: Make 3 Increase. (K1, yo, k1) into 1 st.

M5: Make 5 Increase. ({K1, yo} twice, k1) into 1 st.

m: meters

mm: millimeters

M1R: Make 1 Right Increase. Lift bar between sts from back to front with the left needle and then knit through the front of it with the right needle.

M1L: Make 1 Left Increase. Lift bar between sts from front to back with the left needle and then knit through the back of it with the right needle.

M1-p: Make 1 Purlwise Increase. Lift bar between sts from front to back with the left needle and then purl through the back of it with the right needle.

oz: ounces

patt: pattern(s)

p: purl

p2tog: Insert needle through next 2 sts as if to purl. Purl together.

p3tog: Insert needle through next 3 sts as if to purl. Purl together.

pfb: purl into front and back of stitch

pm: place marker

rem: remain(s)(ing)

rep: repeat(s)(ing)

Rev St st: Reverse Stockinette stitch (see Techniques)

rnd(s): round(s)

RS: Right Side

S2KP2: Slip 2 sts together to the right needle as if to knit, knit the next st, then pass the 2 slipped sts over.

sl: slip

sm: slip marker

ssk: slip, slip, knit. Slip 2 sts knitwise, one at a time. Insert left needle through front of sts from left to right and knit together.

sssk: slip, slip, slip, knit. Slip 3 sts knitwise, one at a time. Insert left needle through front of sts from left to right and knit together.

st(s): stitch(es)

St st: Stockinette stitch (see Techniques)

T2B: Twist 2 Back. Slip 1 st to cable needle and hold to back. K1 from left needle, then p1 from cable needle.

T2F: Twist 2 Front. Slip 1 st to cable needle and hold to front. P1 from left needle, then k1 from cable needle.

T3B: Twist 3 Back. Slip 1 st to cable needle and hold to back. K2 from left needle, then p1 from cable needle.

T3F: Twist 3 Front. Slip 2 sts to cable needle and hold to front. P1 from left needle, then k2 from cable needle.

T4B: Twist 4 Back. Slip 2 sts to cable needle and hold to back. K2 from left needle, then p2 from cable needle.

T4F: Twist 4 Front. Slip 2 sts to cable needle and hold to front. P2 from left needle, then k2 from cable needle.

tbl: through the back loop(s)

tog: together

w&t: wrap & turn (see Techniques)

WS: Wrong Side

yd: yards

yo: yarn over

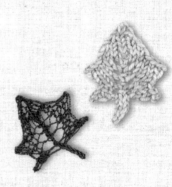

Juniper Moon Farm *Moonshine*
used in *Flourish* { p.22 }

Berroco *Ultra Alpaca*
used in *Ferns* { p.54 }

The Fibre Company *Meadow*
used in *Hanging Leaves* { p.66 }

Becoming Art
Theia MCS Sport
used in *Ivy Trellis
Hat* { p.70 }

Quince & Co. *Owl*
used in *Sprig* { p.12 }

Sunshine Yarns *Merino Sport*
used in *Sunlit Autumn*
{ p.42 }

Becoming Art
509.499.2252
lisa@becomingart-handmade.com
becomingart-handmade.com

Berroco
1 Tupperware Drive, Suite 4
N. Smithfield, RI 02896
401.769.1212
info@berroco.com
berroco.com

Brooklyn Tweed
info@brooklyntweed.net
brooklyntweed.net

Juno Fibre Arts
info@junofibrearts.com
junofibrearts.com

**Kelbourne Woolens
(Distributor for The Fibre Company)**
2000 Manor Road
Conshohocken, PA 19428
484.368.3666
info@kelbournewoolens.com
kelbournewoolens.com

**Knitting Fever, Inc.
(Distributor for Juniper Moon Farm)**
PO Box 336
315 Bayview Avenue
Amityville, NY 11701
knittingfever@knittingfever.com
knittingfever.com

Madelinetosh *Tosh Merino Light*
used in *Forest Foliage* { p.76 }

Brooklyn Tweed *Loft* used in
Twigs and Willows Mitts { p.60 }

Rowan *Felted Tweed Aran*
used in *Bare Branches* { p.32 }

117

Spincycle Yarns
Dyed in the Wool
used in *LIfe Cycle* { p.88 }

Madelinetosh *Tosh DK*
used in *Verdure* { p.100 }

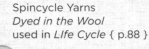

Juno Fiber Arts *Pearl*
used in *Thicket* { p.94 }

Shibui Knits *Cima*
used in *Hanging Leaves* { p.66 }

Shibui Knits, LLC
1500 NW 18th, Suite 110
Portland, OR 97209
503.595.5898
info@shibuiknits.com
shibuiknits.com

Spincycle Yarns
1318 Bay Street, Room 200
Bellingham, WA 98225
360.752.0783
spinster@spincycleyarns.com
spincycleyarns.com

Rowan Yarns
Green Lane Mill
Holmfirth
West Yorkshire
England
HD9 2DX
+44 (0)1484 681881
knitrowan.com

Madelinetosh
7515 Benbrook Parkway
Benbrook, TX 76126
817.249.3066
info@madelinetosh.com
madelinetosh.com

Quince & Co.
info@quinceandco.com
quinceandco.com

Sunshine Yarns
info@sunshineyarns.com
sunshineyarns.com

And thanks to all of you amazing knitters out there for being so wonderful and supportive...

acknowledgments

I would like to acknowledge and thank the following contributors who helped make this project possible.   119

Graphic Design by Mary Joy Gumayagay (indus3ous.com)

Technical Editing by Tana Pageler and Dawn Catanzaro

Illustration by Neesha Hudson (neeshahudson.com)

Photography by Shannon McCabe and Carlee Tatum

Modeling by Courtney Riddle

Test knitting by Andrea Sanchez, Anne Ginger, Ashley Frencl, Cathy Berry, Janet Johnson, Kathleen Moul, Kristen Rettig, Rebecca Swafford, Sarah Cote, Veronika Jobe

Copy Editing by Nicole Crosby (thefinalwordediting.com)

Thank you to my husband, Jason, and the rest of my family for your continued support.

and for allowing me to have the best job ever. I am so grateful.

tiny ivy

These *Tiny Ivy* leaves can be knit in the yarn of your choice at any gauge. They are adorable all on their own, but you can also knit several at a time to string together for a craft project. There are endless creative possibilities.

Enjoy!

CO 3 sts. Work in I-cord for 5 rnds total.
Next row (RS): K1, yo, p1, yo, k1, turn. 5 sts.
Row 1 (WS): P2, k1, p2. **Row 2 (RS):** K1, M1R, k1, yo, p1, yo, k1, M1L, k1, using backwards loop cast on, CO 2. 11 sts.
Row 3: BO 3 purlwise, p2, k1, p4, CO 2. 10 sts.
Row 4: BO 3, k2, yo, p1, yo, k3. 9 sts.
Row 5: P4, k1, p4. **Row 6:** K4, yo, p1, yo, k4, CO 1. 12 sts.
Row 7: BO 3 purlwise, p2, k1, p5, CO 1. 10 sts.
Row 8: BO 3, k2, yo, p1, yo, k3. 9 sts.
Row 9: Purl. **Row 10:** Ssk, k1, S2KP2, k1, k2tog. 5 sts.
Row 11: Purl. **Row 12:** Ssk, k1, k2tog. 3 sts.
Row 13: Purl. **Row 14:** S2KP2. Cut yarn.
Fasten off and weave in ends on the WS.